The Cherokee Paradox

Unexpected Ancestry at the Crossroads of Identity and Genetics

By Christopher "Hodalee" Scott Sewell

Published by Backintyme Publishing

Crofton, Kentucky, U.S.A.

Copyright @ 2016 by Backintyme

Backintyme Publishing

1341 Grapevine Rd.

Crofton, KY 422117

270-985-8568

Website: http://backintyme.biz

Email:backintyme@mehrapublishing.com

Printed in the United States of America

March 2016

Title ID: 6156305

ISBN-13: 978-0939479443

Library of Congress Control Number: 2016936625

THE CHEROKEE PARADOX: UNEXPECTED ANCESTRY AT THE CROSSROADS OF IDENTITY AND GENETICS

BY CHRISTOPHER "HODALEE" SCOTT SEWELL

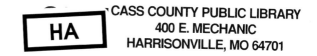

"We know what we are, but not what we may be."

-William Shakespeare

"When I discover who I am, I'll be free."

-Ralph Ellison, Invisible Man

"It ain't what you don't know that gets you into trouble. It's what you know for sure that just ain't so."

-Mark Twain

Contents

Foreword

What creates the sense of identity that we have as human beings?
What are the forces that influence the crafted sense of 'self' that each
of us has? Identity as we have known it looking back to years past
has undergone great changes and if we look ahead will undoubtedly
undergo even greater changes as American society continues its
great experiment in democracy. Race, ethnicity, language, culture,
religion; all these aspects of identity are in a time of tremendous flux
unparalleled in the past. Libraries could be filled with books about
just the measurable statistical changes occurring around us daily in
the exponential diversification of society as we know it.

Living in the information age the impact of easily accessible data
about the world around us is a constant stream of information for
many, usually reinforcing perspectives already held. But a recent
development of our modern data driven lives has upset, not
reinforced, the view of themselves held by some. To get just a snap
shot of this speeding locomotive of social change and its unexpected
complexity as it is hurtling by us faster each day, it's helpful to take
a look at it through a small slice of our American pie; the redefining

of the way many people see themselves when they receive data about their genetic ancestry through newly available and inexpensive DNA testing is one such way to catch a glimpse of that present moment in time, one unique and passing.

With the risk of treading on the precarious ground of race, identity, and history, not to mention politics, I have approached these circumstances which are impacting hundreds if not thousands of people recently with trepidation and curiosity. I witnessed several personal; friends confront difficult personal crossroads of identity. They were average Oklahoma folks one would say. Persons who thought of themselves as "Cherokee Indian", just as their Certificate of Degree of Indian Blood (CDIB) cards said yet when receiving their DNA tests found very little and for some NO genetic American Indian ancestry being found would, without doubt be taken aback by such results, as anyone would. They asked how this could be.

For a few it was an emotional blow and greatly impacting of their view of themselves, for others it was an interesting anomaly and generally irrelevant to their self-view; for most it raises questions as to why their test would show no Indian ancestry. Reactions are from personal relationships as well as others anecdotal stories diverse. One or two chose not to discuss the fact that they had taken such tests at all within our social circle, while others refuted that the results could be accurate. Responses were varied and reflective of the unexpected suddenness of the results for some, often dependent on how vested the person was in the identity they had forged over the years of their life. Years ago long before DNA testing made its appearance in Indian Country a traditional elder who was an enrolled member of Cherokee Nation and from Park Hill told me during a discussion of tribal identity his perspective on being Cherokee Indian.

"Indian is a race; Cherokee is a nation; it is a culture, a language, and a way of life. There's as many ways someone is Cherokee as there are Cherokee."

I have spent many years of my life as a resident of the Cherokee Nation and as such have come to know countless people for whom their ties to the Cherokee people and culture were important parts of their life, for some the most important aspect of their identity. More than any other tribe, the Cherokee are unique, are singular among tribes in many ways. This is something which can be strength, or a weakness depending on how it is perceived. The Cherokee identity is one of the most complex of all found not only among the people of Indian country, but among any who count this continent their home.

While the term "Cherokee Paradox" does not actually specifically refer only to Cherokee people, but more to the phenomenon of persons getting greatly unexpected results from DNA tests, data that for some is completely different than they expected, the term does capture the trend in very subtle ways when Cherokee history and identity is considered, especially as illustrative of the larger ideas of identity and belonging to a group. Though it is among the largest of federally recognized tribes in numbers of enrolled members, it is arguably among those with the least Native American ancestry present in the average enrolled citizen of the Cherokee Nation, judging from the many friends who have shared their CDIB blood quantum amounts with me.

Controversial of a statement as it may seem to those unaware of the intricacies of Cherokee history, in the twenty-first century, MOST of the members of the more than 300,000 strong people of the Cherokee Nation are of MOSTLY European genetic origin; the Cherokee Nation would not be alone in this either, There are many tribes across the country, especially some from the eastern United States and whom have only a minimal amount of Native American ancestry present in modern enrolled members yet who are federally recognized tribes. It's easily observable that many Cherokee citizens today are lacking the physical appearance of the Indian expected by most Americans in their conception of the Indian as imagined. This shouldn't surprise some. To give an example of how strange the identity of many Cherokee are in comparison to other tribes in his scholarly article "The Racial Paradox of Tribal Citizenship", Cherokee Steve Russell states that the continued exogamy by the vast majority of Cherokee citizens leads the Cherokee Nation to claim citizens of 1/2048 blood, indeed eleven generations from a full blood Cherokee ancestor (Russell, 2006).

This difference in the actual Cherokee community and Indian tribes as conjured by the American imagination, much less realities of social units is in some degree due to aspects of Cherokee history which due to its inclusive rather than exclusive way of life accepted large amounts of non-Indian people into the Cherokee community from the earliest days. The images of the Indian as imagined by the media for a century now has also played a large roll in forming the average Americans largely created concept of "the Indians." As anyone who looks into the recent and historic experiences of the Cherokee Nation, this inclusivity has not impacted the resiliency or identity of the tribe as one may expect, but could well be argued to have had a strengthening effect on the Cherokee Nation as a whole.

Today the tribe is doing well and its members can be proud of the accomplishments of Cherokee Nation since its arrival in the west after the tragedy of the Trail of Tears in the 1830's. While on a national, cultural, and social level the members of the Cherokee Nation have for the last few decades been enjoying a renaissance of sorts, renewal after the cultural erosion and legislative attacks on tribally based institutions and identity by the state and federal government a century ago; today a new aspect in the ongoing narrative of the formation of Cherokee identity has developed as DNA has given a new stream of data for those interested to ponder. This new vista of ancestors long gone that is opened up through the use of modern genetic testing techniques is one that is replete with revelations of unknown journeys, wars, love affairs, and efforts at social mobility that no archival document could reveal.

There is an unexpected phenomenon which has recently come to the fore with the growth of the emergence of genetics; people who have lived their entire lives believing themselves as primarily belonging to a specific ethnicity or race and who upon taking newly-available inexpensive Direct to Consumer (DTC) DNA test find that it identifies the origins of their ancestors as having little or none of that long-held identity in their background! After this happened to people who were enrolled members of the Cherokee Nation and who contacted leading geneticists and companies about what they thought were possible errors in the data, it came to be known as "the Cherokee Paradox" by some. The phenomenon is in no way restricted to people with Cherokee roots though. This situation has now become so common it is even a marketing tool for the DTC DNA testing giant Ancestry.com. As an example of this a recent Ancestry.com television commercial said it best.

The ad showed an individual Ancestry.com customer who had always been told by his family that he was "German" in ancestry and had even gone so far as to join a German heritage dance group and bought lederhosen, (which was initially shown on screen wearing), only to find upon taking the DTC DNA test from Ancestry.com that to his surprise (and no visible consternation) that he was of no German ancestry at all but was of significant Scottish and Irish origins; so he traded in his lederhosen for a kilt he goes on to say as he is shown in his new Scottish garb smiling. For some today finding out that they are not who they thought they were much of their life, the phenomenon from the commercial is not so smooth an affair, especially in the touchy area of Native American ancestry.

In some Indian communities, especially those in Eastern Oklahoma and other areas with large tribal groups, many with tribal members with lower amounts of Indian ancestry than other larger western tribes, many people have their tribal identity and self-perception built upon a small handful of ancestors or even a single Native American ancestor who lived one, two, and in some cases almost three centuries ago. With the remoteness of the ancestors of some tribal members, the dynamics of genetic inheritance come to bear; any ancestors a person has beyond a half dozen generations ago contribute little to any persons genetic makeup, and would in most cases not show up at all in the standard DTC DNA tests many are taking.

Often unaware of this reality, I have as stated earlier counseled several friends who were extremely surprised when they received the results from their tests and found it showed no Native American ancestry despite the Certificate of Degree of Indian Blood card they possessed. The CDIB card and the blood quantum system it represents is one of the most controversial "facts of life" for many Indian people.

A CDIB Certificate of Degree of Indian Blood or Certificate of Degree of Alaska Native Blood is an official document from the United States government. This card certifies that the person has a specific degree of Native American blood, originating from a federally recognized Indian community. Applicants are issued the CDIB by the Bureau of Indian Affairs after they have supplied a complete genealogy, along with supporting legal documentation such as birth certificates and others, showing their descended from an enrolled Indian or an Indian listed on a tribal base roll, such as the Dawes Rolls in the case of Cherokee Nation. It must be noted that a person's blood degree cannot be through adoptive parents.

The blood degree someone had on previously issued CDIBs or on the base roll utilized in the filer's tribal ancestor's blood degree is usually used to establish the applicant's blood degree. A CDIB card forwards only the blood degree of one tribe or the totality of the blood degree from all tribes in the applicant's Indian ancestry. As certain tribal groups demand a specific minimum degree of that's tribal ancestry for enrollment with them, a position which might require the first type of certificate, some federal government benefits programs have standards which entail a minimum total Indian blood degree, and in this case some might require the second type of certificate for inclusion. The issue is far from simple as you can see.

There a countless hundreds of examples of this complexity but for an example close to the subject at hand, the Eastern Band of Cherokee

Indians in North Carolina provide one. The Eastern Band require at least 1/16 degree of Eastern Cherokee blood for tribal enrollment' though the Bureau of Indian Affairs' Higher Education Grant for university expenses require a 1/4 degree minimum. We will look in a future chapter more in-depth at the Eastern Band of Cherokee and controversies relating to their enrollment. Surprisingly too many, a Certificate Degree of Indian Blood by no means establishes membership in a tribe, since a tribes enrolled membership is established by tribal laws, and the tribe may or may not require a CDIB, or could call for a separate tribal determination of blood degree.

The CDIB and the blood quantum system are controversial and divisive in the view of some, and from a racial politics perspective of its impacts, its tangled governmental machinery looms over the lives of many in Indian Country, where it defines them and their access to tribal resources tangible and intangible. Non-federally recognized tribal groups, of which there are hundreds, are not eligible for the CDIB card or for the benefits which require one to access. Some groups, such as the Cherokee Freedmen which we will examine closer later in this work, are not eligible for a CDIB because they are not Indian by blood, though they were at one time a people wholly of the Cherokee Nation, the ancestors of many of them held as slaves by Cherokee.

As a group they sought to use genetic data to verify their assertions of the amount of Indian ancestry they possessed. The strategy backfired when many actually had much less, Indian ancestry than assumed by many, especially themselves. The revelations provided by genetics about ourselves and our forebears are coming hard and fast, and some communities, such as the ones already discussed are finding it is more complex than initially assumed. To utilize DNA to try to prove a point conceived before the results are known has real risks as many are now finding out.

The intricacies and somewhat harsh realities of genetics, when it crosses paths with the well-established mores and assumptions of the genealogical and blood quantum methods of the past, guarantees that for many people, surprises abound upon getting the results of the DNA tests. Indeed, the probability for any of us having DNA from all of our genealogical ancestors of a particular generation becomes increasingly small very quickly with each passing generation. To put this into perspective, though there is a 99.6% chance that you will have some small genetic inheritance from each of your 16 great-great grandparents, but there is only a 54% chance of you sharing any DNA with all 32 of your G-G-G grandparents, and a miniscule 0.01% likelihood for your 64 G-G-G-G grandparents.

Important to remember, **a person only has to go back 5 generations for genealogical relatives to start dropping off your DNA tree**. This is the crux at the root of the Cherokee Paradox, as the systems used to track 'Indian ancestry' by blood quantum is not rooted in the realities of genetic inheritance. Having Indian (or any particular) ancestry for certain, beyond ones grandparents, grandparents is a very improbable, and touchy proposition.

The impact of the advent of easily accessible genetic information on the controversial situations relating to identity in Indian Country is still unfolding, but is by no means restricted to Native American communities as I have said, but the playing out of the impact of this phenomenon in Indian Country is illustrative of the larger impact across American society as well. Genetics are truly bringing a new dynamic to the search for identity long pursued by many Americans of all backgrounds. Like genealogy, it has its strengths and weaknesses, but it offers insights into our origins with a certainty that the hours spent in genealogical research cannot. In this work let's look at a few of the issues surrounding the unfolding new world of Direct to Consumer DNA testing and its impact on identity.

Genetics: A New World of Information

Genetics has a reputation as a subject as being complex can be initially daunting, but some basics of the field can help us be oriented to this exciting and cutting edge area of science, that once examined is not as complex as one might think. As we all learned in 6th grade Science class,(if we were awake that is), we share half of our genetic material with our mother and half with our father, and also each one of us shares half of our genetic inheritance on average, with our siblings. As our close examination of the color of a babies eyes or the size of grandpa's nose often reveals, families indeed share significant genetic ties to one another. Siblings are inheritors of half the genetic contribution from their parents[1].

The fewer genes we have in common with someone the more distant the family relationship between us. That a quarter of our DNA is shared with each of our four grandparents, as well as our aunts and uncles are most likely why my little brother has my grandfather's big ears! Each passing generation our genetic likeness continues to drop by half, becoming less with each increasingly distant branch in the family tree. Each and every person has their DNA coiled into 23 pairs of chromosomes, found in every cell of our body. This gives us 46 chromosomes altogether though there are a few exceptions. The

---

[1] Identical twins are different though and are an exception to the rule as they share their entire DNA between them.

egg cells in women and those of sperm found in men contain only a single copy of each of the 23 chromosomes, having one half of each pair.

As we may remember vaguely from Science class a process called recombination occurs before the pairs get split apart in the eggs and sperm. This process of recombination exchanges DNA between the matching chromosomes of each pair. There are small differences found in a person's genes, so DNA swapping circulates these small differences, creating chromosomes inside the eggs and sperm with unique combinations of genes. The 23 chromosomes located in the mother's egg and the 23 chromosomes inside the father's sperm join together which results in a baby with an entire set of 46 chromosomes. The resulting baby shares half its genes with its mother and half its genes with its father.

Each person is as we have said, 50% genetically related to our siblings, yet the reason for this is different and brings statistics into our inquiry. Just as you, your brother or sister inherited 23 chromosomes from each of one of your parents but their chromosomes have a different combination of genes than yours because of the DNA swapping we have discussed already. Despite this though, half of the genes are still the same, because as we said earlier we have two copies of most of our genes and due to this parents can transmit either of their two copies to you and your brother or sister.

Genetics: A New World of Information

An exercise we did once in Science class helps to illustrate the way we inherit our parents DNA. As we have said you have your parent's genes, as copies of each of their genes were shared with you. Yet as my long ago teacher said, your chances of inheriting from one or the other is easiest compared to flipping a coin. Getting a head or a tail when flipping a coin is totally random, much like in getting our parents DNA in some ways; it can go either way. As each person will have 25,000 genes in our DNA, the question as to if we inherit the "head or tail" of each gene is akin to flipping a coin 25,000 times. We are most likely to get 1/2 heads and 1/2 tails if we did that.

As we each inherit 1/2 heads and 1/2 tails from our parents, your siblings do as well. This being the case, it could be said that you and your sibling are about 50% genetically related, though this isn't exactly accurate. Each of you may not have precisely 12,500 each; you might wind up with 12600 heads and 12400 tails while your brother or sister had 12550 tails and 12450 heads. Whatever the results though except for extremely rare cases you would each get fairly close to inheriting 50%. In short this is the process that leads to you being, well…uniquely you!

What is meant by DNA testing?

DNA testing as used commonly has become a catch-all term to some degree. It most often will refer to various kinds of genetic testing now available that provides information about a person's genes. Our DNA is found in almost all the individual cells in our body, and it is a true roadmap of who we are; our DNA, if present, is exactly the same in every cell in our bodies. This has few exceptions such as any differences that occur by errors in copying of the DNA during cell replication, or changes to the code triggered by external factors, such as exposure to radiation. There are many types of DNA tests, and one is called "DNA fingerprinting". This type of test can be used to help provide documentation of biological relationships. These relationships such as those between parents and their children, as well as among other family members are generally well known from paternity cases and the like.

Other kinds of testing use different sources of data to generate information. Some test for our genetic ancestry through the use of specific markers to see how similar a person is to a broader population set. This is primarily based on probabilities drawn from existing databases of research on specific populations and that group's known genetic characteristics.

It must be understood that there is no DNA testing which can "prove" that a person is an American Indian or has ancestry from a specific tribe, per se. What today's genetic testing techniques can present is evidence concerning the nature of the biological relationship between two persons, as in paternity testing. From that solid ground one sallies forth into some degree of assumption in

Genetics: A New World of Information

making assertions. To be clear, there are no unique genes, no "Indian-only" DNA, for individual tribes or for American Indian ancestry in general. Some genetic markers are found mostly in Native American populations research scientists have found, but to say that these markers are unique to Indian people would be untrue. They cannot be used as a tool to solely predict if someone is of native identity.

Foundational to understanding genetics and the best use for modern genetic testing, one must know that in genetic research, data derived is best expressed in terms of probability or a chance of something's likelihood. Analysis of DNA can estimate the probability of two individuals being related, and commonly this probability is expressed as a percentage of likelihood, such as 95.5% as an example. Genetic testing is already well established in certain areas, such as testing for the parentage of a child. In this use, modern genetic testing can establish a very reliable probability estimate, accurate to within a very strong likelihood. To determine if a person is related to others and how, such as grandparents, siblings, cousins, aunts and uncles for example, the probability will be estimated less accurately. This would be in part because of a smaller degree of shared DNA among those who are distantly related. Probability estimates are rendered accurate with greater probability dependent on having a greater number of people involved in the testing.

The Cherokee Paradox

Probably most notoriously well-known to viewers of afternoon television's fine programming such as Jerry Springer and Maury Povich is the paternity tests. These usually compare a child's DNA to those of a suspected parent, to confirm or rule out their relation to the child. These results are usually expressed as a probability. The mathematical likelihood of the genetic relation between the possible parent and child established by the data is a commonly used test for many years now to establish a child's parentage beyond doubt. Done for the most part through DNA fingerprinting, a process that compares specific sets of genetic markers between the two samples, this genetic technique is called Variable Number Tandem Repeats or VNTRs for short.

This process is used due to these markers propensity to remain extremely similar from parent to the child. Used in criminal forensic cases for constructing a case against a criminal suspect, many times based on genetic evidence sometimes left at the crime scene or on a victim, materials such as blood, hair, semen, and the like, this technique is also commonly depicted on television, though the actual process and protocols are infinitely more intricate and time consuming than that shown on television shows by far. Despite the complexity it is a subject that can be understood with a few basic concepts.

By researchers examining many genes from a person and comparing the persons sample to a much larger database of research findings,

Genetics: A New World of Information

this often called "Continental Origin" type of test can establish insights into the relationship between the individual and various groups of people. How different or similar a person's genetic information is to that of people within a larger group based on probabilities is this tests goal and can provide information about it with strong possible likelihood, but they are limited by the data that is available today. If the context is not known due to there not being enough information present in current databases, (as many do not contain much information for particular groups such as American Indians), then the use of the test is somewhat mitigated. Though the database are steadily expanding, Native Americans are some of the least mapped populations so far.

This limitation of the available database and its lack of breadth in the data for context can produce problems for tribal groups and for individual persons. Using this route to seek information is concerning in some cases, since results may not be accurate or in some case may not even be possible to render, because of the given limited availability of information for comparison. The scientific community is fast expanding into new frontiers of data gathering as well as application of this information across many fields. The role DNA is playing is increasingly large and of the many ways to test for genetic ancestry are themselves undergoing fast evolution in both process and use. Methods such as mitochondrial DNA testing (known as mtDNA), Y-chromosome testing, and the analysis of single nucleotide polymorphisms (SNPs) are all delivering important data and making genetics an increasingly important tool for societal change.

Within each cell of our body are two structures that contain our DNA. Both the nucleus and hundreds of mitochondria carry important genetic data. As mitochondrial DNA can only come from the mother, it is within the egg that the mitochondria is contained which will produce all other mitochondria inside the child's cells throughout their body, and the DNA of the mitochondria is identical for the whole of the maternal line for the most part. Every cell in the body is descended from a single fertilized egg, and as a result, every cell has the same DNA sequence, though there are a few notable exceptions to this. A DNA test that examines mtDNA can provide data about a person and his or her biological mother and other maternal, female relatives in that direct line of female ancestresses. It should be remembered that as specific as that information is, it is but a tiny sliver of the information regarding ones totality of ancestors.

All men have a Y-chromosome, an inheritance which comes directly from their father and from the male ancestors before him. DNA of this chromosome has portions that remain identical for the whole of the paternal line through time. Like the mtDNA genetic test, this one that analyzes a male's Y-chromosome DNA could render data regarding the man's biological father and direct paternal, male relatives as well.

Genetics: A New World of Information

Our DNA is composed of nucleotides which vary between people and groups. These variations are called single nucleotide polymorphisms (SNPs for short). These can be common within a group, as well as being found in individual genomes. Cataloguing these SNPs creates an overall profile of sorts of a person's genotype, or their whole genetic makeup. SNPs genetic test utilize statistical probability as a means to estimate the likelihood of an individual coming from a certain region of the world where the SNPs involved are more prevalent. This being said though SNPs tests cannot conclusively prove whether someone is from a particular tribe or not.

Utilizing SNPs to examine a person's genetic ancestry is a type of DNA testing called Ancestry Informative Markers, or AIMs for short. Ancestry Informative Markers transmit important data about a person's likely ancestry and the differences found between human populations from different geographic regions of the world. Research in recent years has attempted to link genes with specific ancestry related to geographical locations.

A New Industry Emerges from the Laboratory

Genetics has been making the headlines lately, in part because of the growing pains of a sometimes controversial industry which it has spawned, the direct-to-consumer (DTC) genetic testing market. DTC genetic testing raises questions involving complex issues of identity as we have learned. In defining how ancestors are defined, how individual consumers will understand and act upon such information, and the impact this new source of data is having on those tribal communities which find the results differ greatly from the image of themselves and their ancestors long held, the horizon for this emerging industry is indeed full of as much controversy as it is potential.

DTC genetic testing has been around on a limited scale for some years now, but has skyrocketed in the past few years. Emerging in a new form in 2007, the launching of three companies (23andMe, Navigenics and DeCodeMe) and their genome-wide scan services created a new world of potential for those seeking insights into their ancestry as well as other areas of genetic import. Almost overnight, people could send in a sample of their DNA and would receive detailed ancestry information, a wide variety of medical risk information based on the latest discoveries in genetics, and access to genetic relatives some never knew existed. The impact of the DTC revolution was widespread. TIME magazine recognized the 23andMe personal genome service as "Invention of the Year." in October 2008. The party was off and running and in the decade since has only gained momentum.

The Human Genome Project was a scientific collaboration of many parties that was completed in 2003. Without question it is rightly regarded as one of the greatest scientific achievements of our time, and worth the nearly 3 billion dollars spent facilitating its

Genetics: A New World of Information

completion. As important as this milestone was though, the work achieved in the years since is truly significant as well. Thanks to new technologies, powerful systems which that have reduced the cost of DNA sequencing to one one-hundred-thousandth of what it was originally, the world of genetic data had become a universe of such.

During the next decade whole genome sequencing will be available to any individual for under $1,000 and the application of the field across multiple aspects of modern life will be a catalyst for exponential change many social scientists believe. Indeed the biggest challenge in the future won't be the sequencing technologies of genetics, but instead the massive cost and difficulty of interpreting the huge amounts of genetic information generated by such inexpensive and in demand services. The question of identity is a thorny one; an eternally central question found across human cultures and history. That everyone seems to feel the need for some way to identify themselves is understandable, especially so in a complex and variable world growing increasingly so by the day.

As central as the question of how we define ourselves is, it's not exactly clear just what "identity" as a concept encompasses. The questions asked by many, such as are identity more about whom you are as a person, right now, or inquiries more about "what" you are in connection to external forces, in the sense of your heritage and cultural background, are difficult. Though culture, religion, and racial or ethnic community origins have historically been important factors used by people to decide what their identity "really" is, the reality seems to be that the more data we have concerning it, the more abstract the idea of a "real" identity becomes.

Possibly due to this, many people focus less on things like their personality or personal experiences and more upon what can best be termed as 'accidents of birth'. If someone whose ancestors lived in some geographic location internalized their identity, in many cases they seem to "identify" with that location and the culture, religion, and community that's found there, to the exclusion of other less perceptible factors. A new and growing player in how people identify themselves has been created by our modern society: genetics. Because of the growing accuracy and the ready availability of DTC genetic testing, a phenomenon that is due in part to geneticist's ability to identify increasingly more genetic markers, Americans are beginning to utilize this emerging technology to find out more about their genetic heritage.

It would seem that with more information available then someone would have more to confirm what they already knew, but to some degree the opposite is happening. It doesn't appear that more information necessarily confirms what people have believed of their ancestor's identities, but that the situation is actually very different, for both biological and philosophical reasons. Biological reasons for accepting ones identity should be considered most solid because they

Genetics: A New World of Information

are the most difficult to dispute. As genetic testing is limited in what it can tell you about your genetic code and the origins of your genes, it should be delved into with great caution and utilized as one among many factors defining of identity.

The previously mentioned tests are basic genetic tests which have been used in the emerging DTC market, the Y-chromosome and the mitochondrial trace specifically. The Y-chromosome, passed down virtually unchanged from father to son tests for genetic markers on this side even as the other tests for genetic markers on the mitochondrial DNA, data passed down virtually unchanged from mother to daughter. This approach is problematic since a person is only going to have one Y-chromosome or one sequence of mitochondrial DNA. We all inherit the information from one of two parents, and from one of four grand-parents, and so on back for countless generations. This being said if you go back 15 generations, the genetic results of these tests are communicating to you something about only one out of 32,778 of your ancestors! This is hardly informative of the totality of your identity, no matter how interesting or unique.

The questions raised by genetic testing and its resultant data and their involvement in the way individuals and communities define themselves going forward are important to understanding the reorientation this information is having on self-identification. Can such data provide a valid basis on which someone can base their understanding of whom and what they are? If you test positive for a genetic marker common to Native Americans, would you be justified in identifying yourself as a Native American? The questions generated by this new possibility are many.

You could have inherited a genetic marker from a single ancestor 15 generations ago, someone who might be the only Native American ancestor you have; that being the case would one out of 32,778 ancestors qualify as a good basis for a Native American "identity"? Such questions are now coming to the forefront as the impact of the DTC genetic revolution is reaching the shores of Indian country. In my own tribal town community within Creek Nation I know of several members who faced personal identity crises on learning the results of the DTC DNA tests they took. The complex and largely unknown history of the countless ancestors that contribute to our personal genomic identity is no becoming present in an all-too-real way for some.

The American experiment has always involved in large part the idea of the potential to redefine one's self, to not be chained by one's own or an ancestors past, and to have the potential to be who one imagined one could be. With more people seemingly seeking to develop an identity in part by relying upon the finding of genetic markers in their DNA are they doing just the opposite? That they instead may unwittingly be buying into some of the premises of the largely discredited eugenics perspectives of genetics bearing responsibility for ones actions is concerning.

Rather than creating a very personal identity, one made through their own relationships, their professional strivings, and the ideas they develop in their own minds in contexts of family and community, it would seem that for some DNA has other meanings than just inheritance. Its use, often by individuals looking to attach themselves to a communal identity they can share with others based upon genetic information which is ultimately a dwindling minority of their heritage, facilitates the past role of the individual as defining of identity to take on a greater role in the American social milieu.

The Direct to Consumer (DTC) Genetic Testing Industry

DTC genetic testing generally refers to a standardized simple genetic test, often in a kit, that are marketed directly to American consumers through television commercials, advertisements in print, or through the Internet. Also known as at-home genetic testing, this new means provides access to a person's genetic information without necessarily involving a doctor or insurance company in the process, unlike those of the past decades. The emerging Direct to Consumer genetic testing industry is transforming the way people who become aware of their genetic roots are seeing their identity, on a personal and social level. Genetic research advances have been growing exponentially and these have led to a new world of information for some, data which often involved unknown facets of their makeup.

Advances in the past decades into the area of genetics have led to entirely new industries, started social trends now becoming standard, and creating phenomenon that are impacting people across the social spectrum. Until only a few short years ago, most of the Direct to Consumer ancestry tests for the average American consumer, those who for the most part interested are in learning more about the continental origin of their forebears, used short stretches of their DNA found in the cell-powering organelles, called mitochondria. Today the methodologies used are more complex, and indeed more telling in the specificity they reveal.

40,000 to 80,000 years ago, as humanity spread into other parts of the globe from our common African homeland, we carried with us specific sets of traits rooted in our genomes, and some mitochondria and Y chromosomes evolved specific changes, transformations that were connected to various human populations. These genetic markers are an inheritance from our forebears. They are an unbroken chain that connects each of us back through time to our ancestors; through the maternal or paternal lines of descent, we are just the most recent generation and these markers are rarely unique to a specific population. The social commentary emerging from this unfolding area concerning racial identity and the question of genetic

Genetics: A New World of Information

discoveries impacting the racial categorical constructs of our past has been front and center for the past several decades.

The importance of the reconstruction of our history and more recent as well as ancestral population migration patterns, revelations which are resultant from the research in the genetic field are now becoming apparent. Often defined by the differences of geographical origins, racial designation or ethnicity, or culturally defined identity, the interrelatedness of populations is many times obscured. Fortunately for us, the "genetic map" allow us to gain insights into the depth of the connections that unite us like none before.

The new insights gained are not without challenges to current social assumptions though. To some degree sociologists have hand their hands full in synthesizing the emerging data into the social paradigms as understood. They have allowed that some of the information resulting from genetic research can serve in some cases to *"tacitly to re-inscribe existing socially determined racial categories"* of the genetics of populations in the mind of the public. Though the use of DNA to answer questions about our common human past has led to powerful revelations about our origins long ago, DTC genetics has facilitated an emerging social dialogue about identity that is 'overturning the tables' in the temple of socially constructed American landscapes in the lives of some.

The Cherokee Paradox

According to global industry analysts, the global DTC genetic testing market is projected to reach the size of more than $230 million by 2018[2]. Searching for our personal recent and ancient ancestral roots is now easier than ever with the current advances in technologies such as the field of genetics and digital genealogical records availability. DTC genetic services can encompass DNA testing for the purpose of revealing continental ancestry, establishing lines of paternity, and regional ethnicity of ancestors. For the most part, these genetic tests use mitochondrial DNA, the maternal contribution, and the Y chromosome data, which is the paternal contribution, as well as genetic markers on autosomes, which provide ancestral information. Together these allow unprecedented insights into the segments of our origins that contribute to the totality that is us. Some industry leaders have emerged in response to the surging demand for DTC testing, and there are several large genetic companies which provide services to the public.

23andMe is one of the largest in the area. This company, which I myself have used, will provide continental, regional, and sub-regional geographical information (amazingly down to 0.1 percent of your genome) about your origins. The revelations from just a simple test can reveal what percentage of your genetic totality comes from

---

[2] Global Industry Analysts. Future of Direct-to-Consumer (DTC) Genetic Testing Market Remains Fraught. PRWeb [Internet] 2012. [2012 June 10]. Available from: http://www.prweb.com/releases/DTC_genetic_testing/direct_to_consumer_test s/prweb9780295.htm .

Genetics: A New World of Information

the Neanderthal[3]! The heavy hitters in the DTC genetics field are investing mightily in its future, financially and scientifically speaking; 23andMe is one of the industry leaders and provides its customers with information on 78 gene-trait associations. Information posted on the company's website relates that 23andMe analyzes only those associations that have been examined and published in peer-reviewed scientific journals.

The company does divide the associations into two categories: established research and preliminary research. Established research associations are defined by them as those that have been confirmed in at least two large studies or "have gained widespread scientific acceptance in the scientific community" to use their words, while preliminary research associations are those that "still need to be confirmed by the scientific community" and "may not stand the rigors of scientific replication." 23andMe according to its website also relies on an editorial team, including three Ph.D. scientists with university affiliations, to make decisions about which gene-trait associations they will ultimately include in the analysis it provides its consumers.

Though there is indeed something of a sensationalist sizzle to the marketing and presentation of many DTC services, the impact that

---

[3] 23andme.com [Internet] c2007-13. [2012 2012 June 7]. Available from: https://www.23andme.com/.

they are having on the approach people are now taking to find answers to the long standing question "who am I" is significant; The days of dusty archival stacks and obscure and difficult to distinguish microfiche are long gone as anyone can gain access to information with a simple and inexpensive DNA test that is irrefutably personal, yet in many aspects universal. More than any other group, the advent of the DTC genetics movement has begun to impact Native America in ways unforeseen even a decade ago.

Human Diversity: One Race with Many Identities

Human Diversity: One Race with Many Identities

The best way to describe human genetic diversity is that it is the genetic differences found both within and among the countless populations of our world. Until recently if someone was seeking insight into their origins, genealogy provided the most information available, and would be reliable for only a few generations before becoming debatable in its reliability. The use of genetic data to reveal insights about our ancestors is now opening an entirely new window into the countless tales of migration, struggle, and accommodation that our genome reveals. Though seeming complex initially genetics isn't so difficult to understand. All populations share a certain amount of genetic similarity, and each one also has unique markers as well.

As we have seen in the previous chapter, polymorphism involves one of two or more variants of a particular DNA sequence, and the most type found most commonly of polymorphism involves variation at a single base pair. Polymorphisms can involve long stretches of DNA, as well as being larger in size. Genetic scientists are studying how SNPs in the human genome to correlate with many factors including disease, drug response, and other phenotypes. The definition of a polymorphic allele is the natural variations in a gene, DNA sequence, or chromosome that has no adverse effects on the individual and occurs with fairly high frequency in the general population, and their use in genetic research has been important. There likely will be multiple variants of any given gene in the human population present, which leads to polymorphism. Many of the genes we have are not polymorphic, with a single allele found in the population. That gene is then said to be fixed. All humans are 99.5% similar to any other humans on average. These fixed genes allow measurements to be taken and insights gained into our common human heritage.

People across the Earth have always clustered together into like groups, and many times this affiliation with our fellows was then as now most influenced by ones 'phenotypical' appearance. Across the face of our planet human beings look remarkably diverse physically, but an important question is how much of this diversity among humanity is genetically encoded? Today, scientists across many disciplines have been seeking to answer the question of how deeply seated are these differences between the many groups of people. In comparison with many of our fellow mammals, we humans are less diverse genetically. Given our large population and worldwide distribution (of late) this is somewhat surprising, but can be informative.

To look at one of our closest relatives can give some idea of this difference. Humans and chimps share a homeland in Africa that only we humans have recently expanded from, and for anyone who has spent time at the zoo the similarity between our two groups are

Human Diversity: One Race with Many Identities

easily discerned. The chimp as well as another ape, the lesser known but in some ways more interesting Bonobo, are both humanity's closest living relatives. The three species look similar in many ways, both in body type and the behavior they exhibit. To gain insight of how closely all are related, geneticists compare their DNA. A creatures genetic code is made from their DNA, an essential molecule that is basically the instruction guide for 'building' each species. Humans and our cousin the chimp share 98.8 percent of our DNA, making us extremely related branches deriving from the same tree.

Pan troglodytes troglodytes, a subspecies of chimpanzee which are found solely in central Africa, has greater levels of genetic diversity than we modern people, whatever our location! Interestingly, the differentiation between the western and central subspecies of chimpanzees on the genetic level is greater than that found between populations of modern humans! This information may be shocking to some but we and our forest dwelling kin are only separated on the evolutionary scale by a tiny difference, and that these are our closest relative shouldn't be a surprise.

Researchers have found that the majority of genetic diversity among humans is unquestionably between individuals rather than populations or continental groups. Researchers have forwarded that the variation in our human diversity can be best described by geographic gradients, or clines, many early studies of human genetic diversity revealed. To illustrate the point a study that was published in 2004 revealed pointedly that 87.6% percent of the total modern human genetic diversity is found by the differences between individuals. It also showed only 9.2% was discernable between continents. 5%–15% of genetic variation can be found between large groups of people that are living on different continents, and with the remaining majority of the variation occurring within such groups. (Hinds, 2005)

Indeed, when a person form anywhere in the world is sampled, the pattern detected is not discrete groupings; rather it reveals subtle gradients in the genetic variation therein. A gradual geographic variation in allele frequencies is found, a tapestry that extends over the entire population of humanity across our world. To the contrary of treasured ideas held for generations about the nature of social groups, no major genetic discontinuities can be found between the many different groups of people historically found on the different continents or among the socially-constructed "races" that various societies describe. Researchers recently stated their view of race.

"(We) see no reason to assume that "races" represent any units of relevance for understanding human genetic history. An exception may be genes where different selection regimes have acted in different geographical regions. However, even in those cases, the genetic discontinuities seen are generally not "racial" or continental

Human Diversity: One Race with Many Identities

in nature but depend on historical and cultural factors that are more local in nature." (Serre D., 2004)

This being said, the current situation of countless people for the first time gaining insights into their genetic identity is causing some people great surprise when first discovering the tale that their DNA tells about the story of their ancestors. The opportunity to have a window into this fascinating story is coming from the recent advances in genetic sciences and private companies making the ability to gather and interpret the genetic information from anyone fairly inexpensive. In the past, genetic tests have been generally available only through someone's healthcare provider such as their physician, or others. In those days, when a DNA test was necessary, someone's primary healthcare providers would order the appropriate genetic test from a laboratory, then collect and send to a lab their samples, which would be followed by their interpretation of the test results. This is all changed today.

Genetic researchers have used distinct markers from human subpopulations to follow back through countless generations and tens of thousands of years our odyssey into the vastness of the planet from our common African root. On paper this migration fans out from our ancient homeland at the base into a giant human "tree." However, recent developments suggest a "trellis" model might be more appropriate description of our ancestral origins long ago. The ongoing study of our human genome has added a new layer of data, a new chapter of evidence to the story of how we human beings evolved and migrated. All people are far more similar than they are different; while the evolutionary changes in our genome itself are difficult to tease apart, because of having been shuffled and reshuffled countless times throughout our history. Two mechanisms of genetic inheritance, one being paternal and one maternal, and which do not involve recombination have been valuable tools for understanding the oft complex relationships among human beings from different continents and from different times in human history.

Hidden Ancestries: Are We Who We Think We Are?

Hidden Ancestries: Are We Who We Think We Are?

Many modern 'mainstream' Americans with European-American ancestry would guess that they have some African ancestry if asked. This makes sense as most people in mainstream society believe that humanity emerged in Africa and migrated to other parts of the globe tens if not hundreds of thousands of years ago. But the complex realities of ideas about race and how it relates to history have conspired along with human nature to obscure the majority of our ancestor's identities behind a cloud of simplified and largely assumed labels, assumptions, and in some cases lies. Emerson saw our ideas about race in the past as central to America's inherent success, and penned such in 1835.

"The inhabitants of the United States, especially of the Northern portion, are descended from the people of England and have inherited the traits of their national character...It is common with the Franks to break their faith and laugh at it The race of Franks is faithless."

That race as present in America of the twenty first century has a biological element is, as one scholar said, without doubt because we have bestowed it one and willingly maintain it. Race is no more based on the color of a person's skin in our day than it was on "Frankishness" in the time that Emerson's writing captures. The convoluted history of race across generations recent and remote has taken geography, language, and projected traits as its foundation and ran with it wildly across time, space, and lives of our fellow humans.

"Race is an idea, not a fact."

This perspective forwarded by the great historian Nell Irvin Painter remains true today in the eyes of much of the academic community. The debate as to the concreteness of race is one that's raged for years, with little new available data to disrupt the engrained arguments, with the treasured positions solidified long ago safe from being toppled; the border of science and culture was very diffuse in the study of race and identity in the past. Such was the case until with the arrival of genetics as a tool of inquiry; with the arrival of the ability to read our past in our genomes the long held 'sacred cows' of racial identity constructs are rolling their eyes in fearful anticipation of the impact of the data genetics is revealing on society and its origins.

Our genetic identity as inherited from ancestors, distance forbears who lived some 50 to 80,000 years ago when humanity began its planetary expansion, is not measurable through the autosomal DNA tests many are now taking. For the most part these tests only accurately measure a person's more "recent" ancestry, another words our ancestors just over the last two or three centuries. What the recent revolution in DTC genetic tests are revealing is how many "self-identified white" people are finding out today of their recent

Hidden Ancestries: Are We Who We Think We Are?

"hidden" African ancestry in their families. Especially in the American south many are finding out that family history as passed along "left out" some of the story.

According to the notorious "one-drop rule" of the Jim Crow Segregation era, these people would have been considered legally "black" and like some of the Native American communities' of the south experienced the racism of the times. The American classic To Kill a Mockingbird is informative of the experience of some southerners wrestling match with race.

"Well how do you know we ain't Negroes?"

"Uncle Jack Finch says we really don't know. He says as far as he can trace back the Finches we ain't, but for all he knows we mighta come straight out of Ethiopia durin' the Old Testament."

"Well if we came out durin' the Old Testament it's too long ago to matter."

"That's what I thought," said Jem, "but around here once you have a drop of Negro blood, that makes you all black." (Lee, 1988)

In the conversation above, two main characters Scout and Jem share with each other how society divides people, lumping them into races, and the repercussions when those dividing lines break down. Even though only young people, they can see that the "one-drop rule" doesn't really work. Its assumption that unless every drop of someone's blood can be accounted for, or to put it in modern terms the results of their genetic test show as of a singular origin (not very likely), then how could one know without doubt the "truth" of a person's identity? That some so-called "white" Americans today would be classified as "black" under the one-drop rule shouldn't be surprising in the light of modern scholarship into the color line and the struggle to maintain human dignity in the face of external pressures to assimilate into the bi-racial classification characteristic of the legal and social system of the Jim Crow era. Judging by the last U.S. Census that number could be as much as 7,872,702; the number is equal to roughly 20 percent of the total number of people identified as African American in the same census period.

That there are a lot of white people with "hidden African ancestry," especially in the south is a well understood fact within many of these families, even as they have strived mightily to keep this from public attention in the small rural communities where they live. Though these recent ancestors of many "white southerners" were a part of the Black community, paradoxically, their families were able to pass for white in a short amount of time, socially speaking. This is an occurrence that is still happening though more difficult to track in our time. As the moral history of countless families from the Deep South reveal, the notions of ancestral origins are sketchy to some degree. When opportunity was presented, there were many who crossed the color line and established lives in new communities, along with a new racial identity. As Dr. Henry Louis Gates Jr. put it

Hidden Ancestries: Are We Who We Think We Are?

in an interview a few years ago, the escaping of the trap of race was often available to those with some initiative.

"All they needed to be able to pass was a tank of gas and a new destination. Their jumping-off point was the color line itself."

As some members of my own family including my Scott and Williams ancestors did this during Jim Crow, I understand the motivation of family members to do what they could to provide better opportunities for their descendants. The color line has long been a frontier of race and identity, and as Professor Frank Sweet documented in his 'History of the Color Line ', the boundary between the races is extremely porous. Katarzyna "Kasia" Bryc is a Population Geneticist who is a part of the team at 23andMe, a company who I took my own initial DNA test with.

She has developed statistical models which utilize genetic data gathered from various modern population groups to learn about ancient human history and migrations, recent population admixture and other influences that have helped to shape the human genome present today. Some of her research has given a window into this phenomenon, and has revealed important data about the frequency of "hidden African ancestry" of many.

"Southern states with the highest African American populations tended to have the highest percentages of hidden African ancestry."

The Cherokee Paradox

The perspectives revealed in her statement are close to home, as my archival research revealed years ago what the DNA tests I took in recent confirmed. Ancestors crossed the color line, sometimes undetected, for others with resistance from the legal authorities. 23andMe Content Editor Scott Hadly writes of Bryc's findings in a recent post, telling of the realities of southern interracial admixture in the past, incidents exactly like my own family who in large part originate in the Carolinas.

"In South Carolina at least 13 percent of self-identified whites have 1 percent or more African ancestry, while in Louisiana the number is a little more than 12 percent. In Georgia and Alabama the number is about 9 percent. The differences perhaps point to different social and cultural histories within the south."

Many people speak of mixed ancestry they expected to see in the results of their DNA test before they see them, but it's more often a different "mix" than most expected to see that surprises so many on the several television shows now popular. Dr. Gates has found in his research that generally speaking, most Black people usually guess that they have higher percentages of American Indian ancestry and lower percentages of European ancestry than they actually have once they are tested. A similar statement would be true about Whites as well. Many Whites and Blacks both assume more Native American ancestry than is usually present, even while underestimating the degree of other ancestry. Research to date reveals that very few

Hidden Ancestries: Are We Who We Think We Are?

African Americans have significant amounts of Native American in their recent ancestry.

A study published by 23andMe researcher's revealed that only about 5 percent of African Americans have at least 2 percent of Native American ancestry, and showed the average African American has only 0.7 percent American Indian ancestry, an amount usually significantly less than they assumed. On average, African Americans have a significant 24 percent of European origin in their ancestry, no small amount. Recently Professor Gates stated that if the percentages used are extrapolated across to the last federal census they would mean that 487,253, "white" people in Georgia, 385,156 "white" people in South Carolina, 328,186 in Louisiana and 288,396 in Alabama are actually "black," according to the one-drop rule! Professor Gates goes on to say that the percentile of "hidden blacks" who are currently self-identifying as "white" in South Carolina, around 13 percent, is interestingly, the same as the percentage of people across the United States who self-identified as black on the federal census enumerated in 2010. Such data as this, reflective of unknown trends in identity formation, were formerly hidden before the use of modern genetics.

In an article published in The New York Times recently about First Lady Michelle Obama's ancestry, it was found after tracing her maternal line back through the generations that her great-great-great-grandparents were a slave girl and a white man, and their son,

The Cherokee Paradox

Dolphus T. Shields, was born in the 1850s. This isn't surprising since almost sixty percent of the African American population have at least 12.5 percent European forbears. The popular family oral history of Native American ancestry is not proven out, as genetic research shows only 5 percent have as much Native American ancestry. 30 to 35 percent of all Black males can trace their male lineage (traced through their y-DNA) to a white man, and most likely during the period of American slavery.

These roots of people today that reach back into a painful period in American history are often minimized or buried. Indeed, as the 88-year-old woman who attended church with Michelle Obama's great-great-grandfather, Helen Heath put it "people didn't want to talk about that." The oral history of many African-American families make clear that First Lady Michelle Obama's family history are in no way unique, the findings of population geneticists documenting this same history for almost all families in the Black community.

Appearances are misleading and don't give an accurate reading of someone's ancestry. Many Americans think that people who are fair-skinned are thought to have only white ancestry, with anyone who "looks" white are lacking any African ancestry. That Americans have such presumptions is not surprising, as the history of the color line documented by Professor Frank Sweet in several works notes has been constantly moving throughout American history. These ideas of appearances being accurate determiners for the identity of

Hidden Ancestries: Are We Who We Think We Are?

someone racially do go nicely with the America's historic racial paradigm. This view of race allowed the authorities and dominant social order to put everyone into their racial "place" and to decide from that how they should be treated.

Members of my own family learned this in the deep south of the segregation era. The extensive coverage of the tale of the First Lady's white, black and Native American ancestors informs the people of a rather common occurrence among African-Americans. Without doubt most Americans have a latent notion that few African-American who are descendants of slaves held by white men are of mixed racial origins, but DNA brings these realities for all who have ties to this shameful episode in American history to the fore. As Mary Frances Berry, a Geraldine R. Segal Professor of American Social Thought at the University of Pennsylvania and former chairwoman of the United States Commission on Civil Rights put it, "This is true though the one-drop rule made us all black, however fair of complexion."

In her family on my father's side, one grandfather was descended from a white slave owner and an African-American slave and the other from a Creek and freedwoman, and she has like many descended from those held in slavery wrestled with its meaning as to her own identity and that of all who descend from them, of any color today. Thanks to historian and genealogist Megan Smolenyak's extraordinary research that was featured in The Times article, we know more of the family of our First Family in generations past. These types of research projects allow a window into the past and remind us of whom we are as a people. It also shows the process of our growth and how we became who we are. We are a jumbled people, a product of violent and occasionally loving relations that we are only beginning to unravel. Professor James Gillmer was accurate in his comment shared in the article that "these relationships can be complex."

Condoleezza Rice, the former United States Secretary of State and national security adviser, would be a woman that would be hard to surprise one might think after her many years in government service, but Dr. Henry Louis Gates Jr, the formerly mentioned host of a recent television series on Public Broadcasting called 'Finding Your Roots', did just that when he revealed to her that nearly half of her ancestors could genetically be traced to Europe (an occurrence not uncommon among African Americans). Mrs. Rice, who identifies herself as "an African American", said to Dr. Gates, "I'm stunned." As we are discovering in many communities, often time's persons of mixed ancestry have varied reactions to the revelations revealed by genetic information; acceptance, insight, or minimization are common responses to the data when in some cases completely unanticipated information is revealed.

While minimization, denial, or acceptance is a few of the short term reactions of those who receive unexpected information from their

Hidden Ancestries: Are We Who We Think We Are?

genetic information provider, the long term responses are continuing to be observed. Identification of African Americans with the "African" portion of their ancestry is the most commonly experienced reaction among them, while the European portion of their ancestry is minimized by many, often spoken of as the result of rape of other negative events in the lives of ancestors. With the history of bondage that is foundational to the first Africans to arrive and their descendants, the view is understandable, if not always accurate.

Entire communities of 'Free Persons of Color' were established and thrived in many regions and some continue to even yet. The story of the Africans who first came to this continent and of those who they gave rise to in subsequent generations is truly complex and is not swerved by blanket statements, simple explanations, or sound-bite comments, when seeking to really understand their contribution to the American experience. Reactions like that of Mrs. Rice to finding out that half her ancestors were not who she assumed them to be are almost to be expected in some perspectives, especially when history is figured in.

Less well known is a different example of people's reaction to unexpected genetic revelations; that of various types of "Native" activists, many of who are of more European, or even African, ancestry yet who identify more strongly or even exclusively with their "American Indian" ancestry. This is a phenomenon which has been documented many times, even if these individuals lack genetic, socio-political and cultural links with that ancestry, is interesting and surprising. Many may remember the case of American Indian Movement leader Ward Churchill, and the media sideshow as he was revealed to have little if any documentable Native American ancestry when his genealogical history and ties to tribal communities were examined.

It is revealing of the depth of misguided belief that many people of all 'racial' backgrounds have in their understanding of their family's origins that their frequent surprise reveals in television shows like Dr. Gate's "Finding Your Roots" and others. The surprise they often experience may result from a chosen primary cultural identification with the Native American, African, European of other portion of their ancestry, if they indeed even have such ancestry. The recent case of Spokane NAACP President Rachel Dolezal is one interesting example. In a headline catching event, she was 'outed' by her parents as being 'white', despite living for years as an African American.

In light of the questions about her identity, her background was scrutinized, much like in the Churchill case. Lawrence Dolezal, her father, told a leading newspaper that his theory is that his daughter has long had a diverse group of friends as well as black adopted siblings and she ultimately "assimilated" into the social milieu and culture at the historically black college she chose to attend. He felt

Hidden Ancestries: Are We Who We Think We Are?

that she experienced this assimilation "so strongly that that's where she transferred her identity." After years of debating whether to publicly speak about the complexity of their daughter's social identity, her parents put it simply; "Our daughter is Caucasian".

In contrast to her straight-haired and significantly paler childhood pictures Rachel Dolezal today is a curly-haired, blue-eyed woman who resembles plenty of Americans who identify as black. Despite the passage of time since the incident captured national news, when asked in an interview whether she and her parents were African-American, she had some trouble answering the inquiry simply. Criticisms that Dolezal was in reality raised as a white woman and had at some points in her past formerly self-identified as white, but later had actively and intentionally tried to lead people into thinking she was African American, even to the point of inventing an entire life to suit her story, has left Americans with many diverse reactions to the story. Dolezal's bizarre and complex identity and the maelstrom in triggered has highlighted the strangely unfamiliar landscape of race in America today, and reveals the weakness and malleability of the methods we use to define race.

The experiences of African Americas, like their ancestry, are diverse in the ways they experience race in America. This identification separates them visibly from the other members of the society they live in: i.e., African American people are different to some degree from other Americans because of the African origins of the ancestors they as a people share. For African Americans, the misapplication of their own identity to Africa itself is understandable, due to a lack of knowledge of the complexity of the experiences of the all the persons which contribute to the totality of their experience and identity. An empirical bias lies at the heart of this perspective as it can be safely said that the most phenotypical "African-looking" Americans have substantial European ancestry, and the average for this is near 20% according to some sources.

The opportunity presented by the advent of affordable and easily accessible Direct to Consumer genetic testing for ancestry is that it provides consumers with generally objective data concerning the genetic continental origins of those who came before them. How persons interpret the information provided can vary. Some people react to this information in unforeseen ways, and that response may be viewed as a function of their own psychological constructs and the societal narrative they have inherited concerning their identity. Unquestionably this narrative is in good measure provided by the society they live in.

As knowledge about the new world of ancestral identity that genetic research provides becomes commonplace and a greater understanding of its implication spreads, the place this data has in many different segments of the society will expand, including Native America, which has been the most reticent to participate in many cases. The communities of the past had fewer concretely defined

Hidden Ancestries: Are We Who We Think We Are?

factors available to its members than those present today, and with the tsunami of data available now, the options available to persons in what information they use to define themselves and others will undoubtedly only increase. The hope is that as a whole the American society, indeed the world, will become more enlightened about itself as a totality due to this increased availability of knowledge.

Since according to the 2010 US federal census there were approximately 9 million individuals, (or 2.9% of the population of this country), whom self-identified as multiracial, a large number of people arguably, the growth of the presence of persons of multiracial backgrounds and who identify as such as only grown. We have seen that there is ample evidence that an accounting of the population according to genetic ancestry would produce a significantly higher number. Since so many people live according to the social and cultural identities they have inherited (or created), not ones based on DNA, the numbers reported by the federal census are understandably low. DNA analysis has revealed that as much as 30% of 'self-identified' White Americans have recent sub-Saharan African ancestry, as we have seen many the results of long historical experiences by groups and families considered fringe to the mainstream racial groups of the past.

Examples of the complexity of ancestral journeys and of hidden identities are all around us in our modern society. A tale from the background of the popular actor Johnny Depp is illustrative of this.

The Cherokee Paradox

His ancestor Elizabeth Key Grinstead, born in 1630, was one of the earliest examples of the unfolding struggle for identity in the hothouse of race in the emerging American society. Johnny Depp himself felt the heat of racial controversy when he played a starring role in a recent remake of the 'Lone Ranger', appearing a Tonto, a role which was heavily criticized by many commentators for its inaccurate portrayal of a Native American.

Depp's forbearer was one of the first women of African ancestry in the American colonial communities to sue for her freedom from being held in bondage and win. Elizabeth Key secured her freedom as well as freedom for her small son John Grinstead on July 21, 1656 in the colony of Virginia. She brought forth her case for being emancipated based on the fact that her father was an Englishman and additionally that she was a Christian. Using these two factors as the foundation for their petition, Key's British attorney (as well as common-law husband) William Grinstead successfully petitioned that she should be free. This was an important case, since this lawsuit from 1655 was one of the first "freedom suits" brought by a person of African ancestry in the American English colonies[4].

Its impacts were far reaching since in response to Key's suit as well as other challenges, a law was passed that established the status of children born in the colony would follow the status of the mother,

---

[4] Mario de Valdes y Cocom, "The Blurred Racial Lines of Famous Families: Greenstead, Grinsted, Grimsted, etc.", PBS Front Line, WGBH, 1995-2011.

Hidden Ancestries: Are We Who We Think We Are?

"bond or free". For the status of a child to follow the mother rather than the father, the precedent in English common law, and most often the case in England, was groundbreaking. This law that in 1662 the Virginia House of Burgesses passed, one that would have a ripple effect across time laid a foundation for future decisions and established law.

The principle of partus sequitur ventrum, also called partus, was soon established, and the legislation solidified the framework of the emerging institution of slavery. It did this by ensuring that all children of women slaves, regardless of paternity, would be kept as slaves for labor unless explicitly freed. Johnny Depp is Grinstead's descendant and the experience he had in the roll of Tonto and the backlash to it is some commentary on the central and controversial racial identifies and the depiction of it has maintained in America across the centuries[5]. Reactions by some famous people to their DNA tests results showing their unexpected ancestry is easily extrapolated to many today.

Mark Shriver is another example of the unknown ancestors making a sudden appearance in an unsuspecting descendant's life thanks to DNA testing. Shriver, who is a 'self-identified' white population geneticist at Penn State, revealed in interviews how surprised he had been by his own tests results. These test results which had come

---

[5] "Unmasking The Lone Ranger's Leading Men: Finding the Real Life Heroes in Hammer and Depp's Family Trees". Ancestry.com. Retrieved January 14, 2015.

back 86% European, 11% sub-Saharan African, and 3% Native American were completely unexpected by himself or his family members. The lingering effects of the past racial stigmas attached to specific identities in the eras past are telling in how his mother wanted him to stop publicizing the results of his test, most likely due to consideration of the family's social reputation.

Another person who was televised learning for the first time of their mixed racial background was Oprah Winfrey, The famous talk show host said that she didn't believe that she had any European or Native American ancestry, yet to her surprise her DNA test showed her ancestry to be 89% sub-Saharan African, 8% Native American, 3% East Asian, and 0% European. Quincy Jones, like Oprah Winfrey was surprised at finding results rendered from his genetic test very different from what he had supposed his ancestry was: Mr. Jones' DNA test showed his ancestry to consist of 66% sub-Saharan African, 34% European, and no Native American ancestry, something very surprising to Q, since because of family stories, that he assumed he had Native American ancestors.

These cases from the headlines and television shows are only a tiny example of the crashing tsunami of genetic reality on the shores of the American identity. People like Johnny Depp, Quincy Jones, Oprah Winfrey, geneticist Mark Shriver, and Dr. Gates are today more informed about the origins of their families thanks to genetics and the ancestors who, for whatever reason were in past generations

Hidden Ancestries: Are We Who We Think We Are?

'hidden' are now finding a place in the hearts and minds of their descendants.

They Come to America: Making of an American Identity

In generations past it required countless hours in archives, courthouses, and cemeteries to gain even a small amount of insight into the past lives of ones ancestors. Formerly, the legal, social, and historic identity of our predecessors was rooted in the study of the spotty paper trail left behind, for us to dig out of the mass of the historic record. The legacy they created in their time and lives that they lived are communicated though not only in the documentation found in these archival records, but is now speaking as well from our own genes. The historic record is still providing a unique perspective for us of those who came before, especially now when viewed alongside the genetic data emerging daily. 'Genetic genealogy' is now taking off with promises of vast amounts of data permitting fresh perspectives of the past. From the time when the United States was still a colony of the British through until today the flow of immigrants to this country is still flowing strong. How do we know what we know about those who came before us? In the years past the historic archival records were our main source.

The federal census has always been one of the most important sources of information about our forebears, and informs us of this countries diverse origin of people from across the globe and details of their lives once they became residents of this country. British colonial authorities previous to the War of Independence conducted

47

The Cherokee Paradox

limited censuses in some of the original Thirteen Colonies that included enumerations by race of the person counted[6]. In addition to these important documents, colonial tax lists and other such reports also provide us with general data and some specific information about the racial makeup of the American Colonies during this time period in our country.

The federal census has always been an important part of the American experience and people have been counted in every United States Census since the first one in 1790, and each included the race of the person as perceived by the enumerator, for the most part. Though the gathering of information on race and ethnic identity in the United States Federal Census has evolved over time, changes which include the frequent addition of new enumeration categories and amendments in the definition of those categories meaning, it has always been conducted as mandated except for only a couple of times in American history.

The concept of race as we conceive of it has fairly recent origins. Its perception as a rough division of human populations has a complicated and arguably controversial history rooted in Europe's past. As the usage of the word race is itself a modern term, most generally used in designating of a "nation, ethnic group" during the

---

[6] U.S. Bureau of the Census, Historical Statistics of the United States, Colonial Times to 1970, Bicentennial Edition, Part 2, Series Z 1–19. Chapter Z: Colonial and Pre-Federal Statistics. Washington, D.C., 1975.

They Come to America: Making of an American Identity

16th to 19th century, it must be 'unpacked' to some degree. It came into common usage from the field of physical anthropology from the middle of 19th century forward. Early enumerators of the Federal Census had a difficult challenge in the task of fitting the growing diverse population of America into a few roughly defined racial groups. Most often this boiled down to a white or black classification based on the enumerators perceptions of the identity of the person and instructions they received from the Bureau about what information was to be gathered.

The Black population was extremely small in the American colonies in 1610, but it rapidly grew after this. This expansion in the numbers of African peoples in the Americas expanded with the growth of the slave trade in European colonial areas, many of which would one day became parts of the United States. People of African ancestral origins made up almost one-fifth of the United States population in 1790, but the percentage of population they were would be less in almost every Federal Census until the 1930's. With its history of agriculture and slavery, it should come as no surprise that nearly ninety percent of the African American population lived in the southern portion of the country from about 1790 until the start of World War I, when the trend would change with the Great Migration to north commencing.

The Cherokee Paradox

Previous to the Civil War, the overwhelming majority of people of significant African ancestry were held as slaves in the south. The Great Migration as it became known as was a massive movement of people; one of the largest in American history and which would last throughout the twentieth century resulted in more than six million African Americans journeying north and to a lesser degree west out of the Southern U.S. to new lives in other regions.

This migration, especially from agricultural rural areas and to industrialized urban areas in the northern states was due to the exponentially greater economic opportunities available to the migrants found there. That there was a smaller amount of racial segregation and less blatant discrimination in the northern states was also an important factor leading many Black people to leave behind homes and communities that their families had lived in for generations for the hope of a better life up north.

Though persons of primarily European ancestry have historically made up the overwhelming majority of the total United States population, somewhere between eighty and ninety percent by most estimates, the future appears to harken great changes to come. The United States has been for the most part historically perceived as a European derived country historically; with few "Hispanics", persons of Asian origin, and Native Americans in comparison to the vast body of Americans of significant or solely European ancestry. This assumption was especially true before the late twentieth

They Come to America: Making of an American Identity

century, when great changes in the patterns of population identification began to take place, a trend which is continuing.

The accelerating diversity of the racial and ethnic makeup of the United States is quickly changing, with newly arriving immigrants from Asia and Latin America finding new opportunities here. These immigrants have contributed significantly to the cultural and phenotypic diversity in the American population in recent decades. This remixing of the American body is nothing new, as waves of immigrants from Southern and Eastern Europe did a hundred years ago, and migrants from Northern Europe and Africa did a hundred years before that. Traditionally held boundaries between racial and ethnic groups are swiftly eroding across the American social spectrum, being broken down by high rates of intermarriage as well as a significant growing number of people identifying with their mixed racial ancestry publicly.

Some observers of the social milieu see a "new melting pot", a phenomenon in some corners referred to as the "browning of America". This phenomenon is sometimes described as being characterized by a continued softening of once-distinct racial and ethnic divisions accepted by most Americans as the norm. This perspective of the recent trends in American society forwarded in many narratives is consistent with the idea of the steadily declining significance of race and ethnicity in the lives of contemporary

The Cherokee Paradox

Americans living in the "mainstream" of society. In the view of some though a new grouping of racial divisions are being created as some immigrant groups are allowed to integrate into an expanded (and privileged it should be said) definition of the white population, even as other immigrant groups are not included.

These groups, perceived by some researchers as being "racialized" and subsequently placed socially as disadvantaged brown and black minorities, are a focus for current dialogues on social justice and the constructs of identity in American society. These conflicting perspectives and approaches to identity result because of differing ideological positions on social identity, as well as because the racial and ethnic identities of some are not mutually exclusive and are in many ways fluid; the process of finding their place in the rough and tumble social order of America is one that for some is being negotiated day to day.

So-called "non-Hispanic whites" will be the majority of the population for only a short time more, no longer holding the place it has had historically by 2042, According to data from the US Census Bureau. How the racial pie is sliced is important in understanding these trends though, since many accounts of these forecasts by the mainstream media often neglect to report that whites (as opposed to "non-Hispanic whites" will remain the largest majority for much longer, and are forecasted to be close to two thirds of the US population in 2050 by some.)

They Come to America: Making of an American Identity

As any historic researcher knows though the federal Census Bureau projections by race of the individual enumerated are inaccurate to say the least in some cases, and often to general to be of great use in others. This is because they discount or undercount the generally high levels of intermarriage between persons of various backgrounds, as well the many variations in the racial, social, and ethnic identities of people of mixed-ancestry, the descendants of previous era's social shifts. It is a safe assumption that American population projections by race are somewhat dependent on the self-identified classification of enumerated persons who may have multiple racial and ethnic origins for their ancestry.

By the middle of this century, about a quarter of Asian American people as well as African Americans will both have recent mixed racial ancestry, and more so will be the Latino community; nearly half of all Hispanic Americans will be of recent mixed ancestry, to say nothing of the massive racial social hybridization between Europeans and Latin American indigenous peoples that occurred in centuries past in the homelands of most Hispanic Americans ancestors.

The significant changes in the way persons identify in conjunction with other social factors will greatly influence the way Americans identify themselves and others racially. It should be expected that with growing levels of racial and ethnic mixing occurring and an increasing appreciation for and awareness of persons of multiracial ancestry, the current trends will undoubtedly continue the erosion of customary racial and ethnic divisions in the decades to come. As people from tribal communities well know, many Americans have complex identities, ones that reflect complex ancestral lineages and layers of historical experiences. Any one person is a product of an unbelievably complex process of identity formation. Currents of identity can carry through generations, often being influenced by historic events, tribal and communal origins, community perspectives on race and culture, and historic experience as group.

Though most persons don't change their ethnicity as a matter of course, they may put some heavier emphasis on different aspects of their identity depending on the social circumstances they find themselves in. For instance, a person who identifies as Cuban among relatives may identify as Hispanic when on the job and as American when travelling abroad. In some cases the legal, social, and racial identities of an individual may vary greatly, as someone of mixed ancestry might be viewed as a Native American in one context, but African American in another.

Americans are descendents of people from many varied geographic, ethnic, and racial sources, and the roots of many are scattered globally. Despite their being strong sanctions against interracial relationships and especially intermarriage, there is a great quantity of historical, literary, and now available genetic evidence of ethnic and

They Come to America: Making of an American Identity

racial mixing among all of the peoples who have come to live in the United States; even so many Americans for differing reasons often downplay the complexity of the identity of Americans. While many may be unaware of this reality of the disparate origins of most Americans, many more find it easier to engage in a process of "selective identification" with particular groups of ancestors over others, a practice that over several generations can lead to a significant lack of understanding of the complexity of their identity.

The colonies and subsequently the United States was a multicultural stew from the beginning. Initially the frontier societies were composed of multiple founding populations, with the original American colonies which were formed during the seventeenth and eighteenth centuries accepting many immigrants to their shores on arriving on the American continent, Europeans were of course met by Native Americans, the indigenous peoples of North and South America. These groups were impacted significantly during this era, and many became gradually displaced from their tribal homelands or were absorbed into newer communities by the more numerous European colonists who flowed into the region, oft times being coopted into the indentured servant underclass of the early colonial era. Many of these hybridized peoples would found their own communities, many tri-racial in their genesis but coming to hold a position as a third race in regions where Native tribal groups were extinguished.

With time, many Africans were imported to be utilized as slave labor, being transported to America from the Caribbean and West Africa. Though slavery was the vehicle most experienced as their route to the United States, there were some who did arrive as indentured servants on terms similar to whites in the years of the early colonial period before slave codes were established. Though in the earliest times in the American colonies some Africans had become free people of color, but by the close of the seventeenth century, slavery and being of African ancestry had become nearly one and the same.

Due to imbalances between the male and female populations in the colonial settlements, large populations of persons of mixed ancestry soon evolved, particularly in the colonies of the American South. It is well known that exploitation of black women by white slave owners was a widespread phenomenon and though some of these interracial unions were consensual, many were not. The results of the those relationships from eras gone by today surfacing as hundreds of thousands of 'white' southerners look in disbelief at the results of their DNA tests that show recent African ancestry. As we have seen previously this is no isolated event or one off; the true history of the south and the extent of the intermingling of people of many races is now becoming clear, and it is extensive.

Getting accurate data as to someone's ancestry is highly subjective, as the responses to census questions regarding their race and

They Come to America: Making of an American Identity

ethnicity actually measure identity, something distinct from ancestry, which are the geographic origins of one's ancestors. Overtime disconnect between the two leads to a skewered view of one's origins for many. The origins of a person's ancestors are potentially objective facts; identities of one's self or forebears are subjective articulations of group membership for the most part. Even though ancestry influences identity, its impact is mitigated somewhat by a number of influences. These factors which may include racial admixture, awareness and preservation of knowledge about familial origins, prevailing social narratives about race and culture in one's time, and the amount of time from the arrival of immigrant ancestors to one's self.

The colonial era has much to do with the roots of these communities current genetic diversity, especially for eastern Indian tribes. During the period of American history when slavery was in force in the United States, people were in most cases classified by the enumerated as White, Black or Mulatto on censuses. Complex social hierarchies evolved. Systems of privilege became widespread during slavery, in which Mulattoes were more likely to do household work even as darker complexioned African Americans were more likely to get the difficult and physically demanding tasks outdoors. Often the days of their lives were spent from daybreak to sunset at work in the fields of the plantation.

The Cherokee Paradox

African American identity and the externally imposed "color line" at work in American society have served to defend continuant populations from the hybridizing social forces at work in the American human landscape. The struggles across generations to bring people together in a political and social movement to improve the social position of the community have been unceasing since the earliest of times. The African American community, like the much smaller Native American populations, both peoples who in the Southern states were usually subjected to the Jim Crow laws, has felt constant pressures to be defined externally. Admittedly apart from a limited number of individuals who could "pass" for white, the fate of the many was the fate of the one.

This sense of peoplehood that evolved among the enslaved and their descendents was to become defined in large part by external forces. Sublimated to the greater need for common security and acceptance were the differences amongst community member; overcoming the anger and resentment caused by the different treatment of people primarily based on the varying degree of European admixture was crucial to the integrity of the community, especially in light of its vulnerability to external forces.

Though large portions of the American populace are generally categorized into socially accepted and visibly defined groupings, the subtle variations amongst these are significant, whether the community is racially described as European, African, or American

They Come to America: Making of an American Identity

Indian. The exclusion of a particular set of ancestors and the acceptance of the others is prevalent in Americans. Americans of wholly or predominately European ancestry are no exception to this phenomenon. It's common for Americans to describe their ancestry as for example, French American or Italian American, on the basis of having a grandparent or great grandparent of that origin. The hyphenated identities spoken of as modern American ethnicities are exemplary of this process of exclusive identification with particular ancestors. This process of selective identification with certain lineages of ancestries can extend to entire communities, not only to individual people, and is more pronounced within the Native American community than many.

The book 'Cracker Culture: Celtic Ways in the Old South'[7] makes the assertion that the colonial settlers of the Old South were of predominantly Scots Irish origin. This group is also called the Ulster Scots, and was a significant contributor to the earliest settlers in the American south. According to the perspective of the author Grady McWhiney who wrote the work in 1988, the Northern and the Southern halves of the American social landscape were destined to evolve on divergent paths; each region's unique ethnic roots influenced the subsequent development of its populations. Since the people who settled the North were derived of the stock of the

---

[7] Cracker Culture: Celtic Ways in the Old South. By Grady McWhiney. (Tuscaloosa: University of Alabama Press, 1988)

The Cherokee Paradox

English and the Southerners originated from ancestors of the "pastoral and primitive society" of the Isle's Celtic people, the two regions would logically over time reflect the cultural divide derived from their respective origins.

By examining the activities of the Old South including their culinary, agricultural, herding, and entertainment pastimes and comparing them to his perspectives on pre-capitalistic Celtic society, McWhiney posits that the cultural traditions kept made the Southerners way of life significantly divergent from the more Anglo Saxon oriented industrial and urbanized activities of the North states people. This difference was at the root of the difficult relationship between the two regions, and that the Civil War was almost unavoidable according to his interpretation of the history.

The reality that the southern population, despite factually having a greater degree of immigrants from the Scots Irish population, nonetheless has quite diverse origins with English, Scots Irish as well as German ancestry composing the largest elements, as well as many more streams of immigration from multiple regions . In the spectrum of those primary constituent groups, the English are the greatest in proportion and German the smallest. The inclusion of the significant portion of 'non-white' ancestry, primarily from African ancestors, of the white south of today puts this perspective forwarded by McWhiney as being of limited value in concretely defining the identity of the majority of southerners.

They Come to America: Making of an American Identity

Another example of the past that in some way portended the current changes in the understanding people have of their origins thanks to genetics is a work form decades past is Sinclair Lewis's "Kingsblood", a work written back in the 1947. The protagonist of the work, Neil Kingsblood, ostensibly a white "middle-class" American of the times, finds while researching his ancestors that he is directly descended from a forebear of African origins, an adventurer on the American frontier. Believing he was running down a family tale of a Native American great-grandmother Kingsblood discovers a black ancestor, and his subsequent struggle to come to grips with his identity in some cases foreshadows the experience of several people I know who have met the realities of genetic results unprepared for the results, literally and figuratively.

One would think that in European society, social class would be imposed by the endogamy present among the strata historically, but in the United States, the population sought the "upward mobility" of the American dream, and the resultant milieu would facilitate a more significant degree of intermarriage occurring across the boundaries of social classes. Though this may have been somewhat demonstrable among the portions of the population which composed the mainstream "white" strata, for others it would be difficult to show since the data is existing is extremely small.

Genetic Genealogy: A Powerful Synthesis

Genetic Genealogy: A Powerful Synthesis

Earlier I mentioned the emergence of the new DNA testing trend which is revolutionizing the inquiry into our past. This synthesis of two powerful approaches to research has come to be known as genetic genealogy. This is the utilizing of both DNA testing along with the more traditional genealogical research to gain new insights. Using both DNA data and our traditional approaches to genealogical and historical archival information to infer relationships between ancestors has already had major impacts in clarifying long standing mysteries about forebears for many people. While still somewhat new, genetic genealogy facilitates using the results of genealogical DNA testing to gain deeper insights into the level and familial nature of the genetic relationships between people.

There are many reasons to use the techniques of genetic genealogy but Ill share a few of the most common benefits I have found in it as well as insights from many researchers I know and have heard said they experienced. It is very helpful to learn more about one's specific ancestry especially in a larger social context, and to prove that one's family tree reflects one's actual ancestry, as happened to me several years ago. It is also useful to prove or disprove the relationship between two people, to prove or disprove family lore as to where ancestors came from and their possible ethnic identities.

The Cherokee Paradox

Most helpful it is used sometimes to break down a 'wall' or untie a knot in one's genealogical research. In my own family my mother was adopted and though we have contact with my mom's biological family, there are many people who do not, and genetic genealogy is useful to find relatives for those that were adopted, or who gave up a child for adoption. For children of American G.I. parentage from overseas conflicts this use has been truly helpful in finding family members.

As DNA tests became affordable this use of genetic data became popular with family history researchers. Research efforts by associations such as surname ancestry reconstruction groups, specific regional genealogical clubs, as well as large scale as well as academic research projects such as the genographic project have all seen great results to date. Many hundreds of thousands of people had been tested using the new DNA testing kits from many companies that offer these services today. As the science and its easy application too many areas have developed, the usage of it broadened. It has become popular with many people seeking knowledge of their forbears beyond the recent last couple centuries to which traditional genealogies are limited.

The use of the technique is not new though, as a remarkable study of the past examined the ancestral lineage of the descendants of American founding father Thomas Jefferson's paternal line and male

Genetic Genealogy: A Powerful Synthesis

lineage descendants of his freed slave, Sally Hemmings[8]. Bryan Sykes, the molecular biologist of Oxford University whom authored the work DNA USA which greatly influenced my decision to commence with this work, tested the technique in general surname research in his native British Isles. His research into the Sykes surname garnered results by examining four STR markers on the male chromosome.

This research facilitated the path to genetics becoming an important tool in the investigation of genealogy and historical research. In the last few years the technique has become widespread. Nearly two decades ago now, Family Tree DNA, one of the first companies solely focused on offering to the general public direct-to-consumer testing for genealogy research offered an 'eleven marker Y-Chromosome STR' test as well as HVR1 mitochondrial DNA testing, initially in partnership with the University of Arizona. After this the industry growth was exponential, and it has not slowed since.

---

[8] Slavery at Jefferson's Monticello: The Paradox of Liberty, 27 January 2012 – 14 October 2012, Smithsonian Institution, accessed 23 January 2016. Quote from work: "The DNA test results show a genetic link between the Jefferson and Hemings descendants: A man with the Jefferson Y chromosome fathered Eston Hemings (born 1808). While there were other adult males with the Jefferson Y chromosome living in Virginia at that time, most historians now believe that the documentary and genetic evidence, considered together, strongly support the conclusion that [Thomas] Jefferson was the father of Sally Hemings's children."

The Cherokee Paradox

Brian Sykes research in Britain and his pioneering work The Seven Daughters of Eve, published in 2001, spring boarded into mainstream use personal ancestry testing. This book, which highlighted the seven major haplogroups of European ancestry, stoked interest by many in the area. His book Saxons, Vikings, and Celts was also an acclaimed and informative work and along with other published books give the general reader interesting and anecdotal perspectives on the sometimes bizarre results of our genetic inheritance.

Because of the growing easy availability and its affordable price that anyone could handle, the field grew rapidly. By 2003, the widespread use of DNA testing of family surnames had officially "arrived" with an interesting and informative article published by Jobling and Tyler-Smith in Nature Reviews Genetics. Those who utilized the DNA testing earliest were consumers who most often began with a Y-Chromosome test, which they used to determine their father's paternal ancestry. Reconstructing the branches of a families surname to understand the genetic connections among the various arms of a line of descent gave new and groundbreaking insights often spinning off into even more inquiries.

In my own family I was able to use DNA data about my grandfather's grandfather James Sewell to clarify his biological paternity of my great grandfather, Lark Sewell. This was a relationship which family lore had intimated was one of adoption of

Genetic Genealogy: A Powerful Synthesis

a baby as his own rather than their being a biological relationship between them, as James was called a "helpless cripple" and his census data indicated he was severely limited by his severe arthritic condition lifelong. On taking a DNA test which connected me with hundreds of other descendants of our ancestors across Alabama and Florida where my family has lived for two centuries, I was contacted by a distant cousin from Talladega, Alabama who was a descendent of my great-great grandfather James Sewell's grandfather, seeking information about specific collateral relatives. I was elated to find that this meant that James was indeed the biological father of Lark. After twenty five years of genealogical research with hundreds of unanswered and often unanswerable questions arising, genetics had solved its first case in my research, and it would not be the last.

Prepare for the Unexpected

If you are considering using a DNA test in genealogical research, then you should be prepared for an unexpected result. In other words If you aren't ready for the truth, do not take a DNA test! DNA test results simply reveal what is there and as such doesn't care what we think or want it to say. As an example if someone has a well-documented ancestral lineage and they are positive they connect with ancestor X, but then get the DNA results back and are shocked to discover that you don't match any of the other participants, the repercussions can be shocking. Some genealogist call this a "Non-Paternal Event", another term not as commonly used is misattributed paternity. What this means is somewhere along the lineage the man that was supposed to be the father was not and another males Y-DNA is present in all of the line's male descendants, rather than the ancestor thought to be the founder. Family Tree DNA put it best.

"We believe that the rate of unannounced adoption or false paternity is about 1-2% per generation. When confirming your lineage we recommend that you test yourself and your most distantly related male ancestor to verify the line back to the common male ancestor."

By looking into the past we can get some idea of the accumulation of generations of likelihood of Non-Paternal Events and their impact on our relationship to any specific ancestor. If we use an estimated 30 year span for each generation and a possible 2% Non-Paternal Event rate in 400 years, then there is a distinct possibility that if you are 13 generations from a common ancestor the Non-Paternal Event rate is expected to be about 14%. This is nearly 1 in 7, and no small amount. (Some researchers think the current rate of such events could be as high as 10% with the lessening of social restrictions and the like in recent and modern society.)If we look at some 800 years, about 25 generations of ancestors, then the probability soars to 40% and by 1000 years in the past, or around 35 generations, the possibility of connection to this ancestor is about 50%. The further back in time someone's supposed ancestor, the less likely is that assumption.

Genetic Genealogy: A Powerful Synthesis

DNA Projects

There are currently many people who are using genetics and genealogy together to initiate DNA projects. One of the leaders in this area is the aforementioned Family Tree DNA, whom I have several acquaintances who use their services. They provide three types of projects for people to join. Many are free to get involved in and they are often run by volunteer project administrators. These are usually people who have a specific interest in the topic. There are three kinds of DNA projects for the most part. These are family surname projects which chart surnames like Sewell, Williams, or Kever; Haplogroup Projects which look into haplogroups like R1b, M269 or J1c2f, for both Y and mitochondrial DNA haplogroups and subgroups; Geographic projects which could be said to be any inquiry that isn't a surname or a Haplogroup, for example Lower Alabama or Creek or Irish DNA.

Things to Keep In Mind

In several conferences I have spoken at about genetics and genealogy, someone always asks about the difference, if any, between a person's genetic family tree and a traditional genealogical family tree. The difference could in simple terms be said that your genealogical tree is the family tree that includes all your ancestors. In comparison, your genetic tree only contains those ancestors that actually left DNA to you.

The Cherokee Paradox

In genetics by sheer chance, an individual may not inherit any DNA from a distance ancestor, such as a great-great-great-grandparent, and as a result they would not appear on the genetic tree, even though they are definitely a genealogical ancestor. As we go back in time the relationship to any of our ancestors is complex; with 10 generations passing, I have somewhere around 1024 ancestors (keeping in mind that depending on the community each ancestor lived in and cultural traditions that influenced their choice of marriage partners, there is some overlap). Many people ask about how many of these ancestors is part of my Genetic Tree? What would be the average amount of an individual's genealogical tree at X generations that is also part of their genetic tree?

With the danger of sounding technical, the simplest answer is if by assuming that each chromosome is passed on to us intact, we would have a 50% chance of getting either one from a pair. If this would occur we would have a maximum of 44 genetic ancestors. This means that the probability of being related to any particular ancestor X generations ago is $1 - (1 - 0.5X - 1)22$. Another way of putting it is that someone would have about 43 genetic ancestors out of 1024 genealogical ancestors after 10 generations! This being said, it is most certainly a bit of an underestimate though since outside of the 'fixed' Y chromosome and the mitochondria, ancestral DNA is not inherited by descendants as whole chromosomes; We know that recombination happens, the process wherein chromosomes come

Genetic Genealogy: A Powerful Synthesis

together and swap DNA, and which mixes up DNA. Through this you have DNA from more than 44 genetic ancestors.

Probability for any of us having DNA from all of our genealogical ancestors of a particular generation becomes increasingly small very quickly with each passing generation. In fact, there is a 99.6% chance that you will have genetic inheritance from each of your 16 great-great grandparents, but there are only a 54% chance of you sharing DNA with all 32 of your G-G-G grandparents, and a miniscule 0.01% likelihood for your 64 G-G-G-G grandparents. Important to remember, **a person only has to go back 5 generations for genealogical relatives to start dropping off your DNA tree**. This is the crux at the root of the Cherokee Paradox, as the systems used to track 'Indian ancestry' by blood quantum is not rooted in the realities of genetic inheritance.

If we viewed our ancestors on a chart, we would see that the number of genetic ancestors starts off growing exponentially, but eventually flattens out to around 125. Remember, that around 10 generations ago, about 120 of your 1024 genealogical ancestors are genetic ancestors. An interesting not, which I always wondered about in regard to the Cherokee and other southern tribes and the matriarchal inheritance of clan and identity in these communities; it seems there is a peculiar effect of the larger recombination rate in females; women are, on the average, slightly more closely related to their maternal line, such as their maternal grandmother, their mother's maternal grandmother, on back than they are to their paternal line.

The problem some face in using genetics in relation to genealogical mapping of ancestral lines not without challenges. One of the big challenges for people who would like to use genetics to get a clearer picture of their forebears is that when mapping Y chromosome and mitochondrial DNA polymorphisms, these will trace only two genetic lineages of a person's family tree, one in which branches double with each preceding generation. Utilization of Y chromosome tracing can connect a man to his father but not to his mother, and connect him to only one of his four grandparents, his paternal grandfather. To go a little further with this example, if we follow this lineage on back it will follow the Y back through time and will connect him to one of his eight great grandparents and one of his 16 great great-grandparents and as we journey deeper back through time in this manner, to 14 generations past and the man will be still be connected to only one ancestor in that generation, and the results from his test wont connect him to any of the other 16,383 ancestors in that generation, all to whom the man is also related to in equal measure, genealogically.

Such ties to remote ancestors are tenuous at best. History has had times when such assertions were made and affected lives. As my own family well knows form the racism experienced in the mixed-blood settlement of Scotts Ferry during Jim Crow segregation, it once took only a single genetic line, even one remote ancestor being of questionable northern European racial purity to disqualify someone from being counted as white in the American south, and in our own time it takes only a single genetic line to connect a person to the royal family in the U.K., or to qualify someone as a member of the Jewish Cohanim.

Though this isn't an in-depth explanation of the countless aspects of genetic inheritance to keep in mind when understanding how it and genealogical research can together better reveal the secrets of our forebears, an additional point that I hope that everyone can get an appreciation for the error of putting too much particular emphasis or personal, emotional, or social investment in the unwieldy, outdated, and contrived systems used to create identity in Indian Country. Community participation is at the root of Native America. The true ties in a community are more to one another, the men and women found at ones left and right, than in remote ancestors who may or may not be much related to us.

Community is in many respects a living organism, the participation of its members the life blood of it. Volumes could be written on this subject. That there remains a patchwork across society of humanity being grouped and grouping together by language, religion, and other general aspects of identity, a heritage of the past that will be changing going forward exponentially, should be reason for paying close attention to our American milieu and the forces shaping identity in our moment.

Genetic identity is defined as a measure of the proportion of genes that are identical in two populations[9]. As the hype of DNA testing's potential to essentially define persons soared a decade ago, a leading researcher in human evolutionary genetics, Dr. Martin Richards, rang the alarm bell against making any spiritual investment in the significance of 'not very meaningful DNA sequences' that are defined from DNA testing.

"Studies of human genetic diversity have barely begun. Yet the fashion for genetic ancestry testing is booming. ... Buoyed by the hype, the private sector has been moving in. ... By tracking the history of genes back through time, geneticists can try to reconstruct the migrations and expansions of the human species. They have no special insight into ethnicity and identity." (Richards, 2003)

Tribe and Identity

In researching issues surrounding the struggle over identity, one researcher Fried brought up some succinct points regarding the problem with the concept of tribe and classification of ethnicity, elucidating three key aspects that anthropological geneticists weigh when analyzing the genetic variation of modern populations (Fried, 1968). Like the socially constructed term "race", to say "tribe" is

---

[9] McGraw-Hill Dictionary of Scientific & Technical Terms, 6E, Copyright © 2003 by The McGraw-Hill Companies, Inc.

Genetic Genealogy: A Powerful Synthesis

somewhat of a typological approach to categorizing human populations based on their language, culture, and political organizational patterns. In his perspective, Fried conceives of tribe as a fluid entity, a body without clear boundaries and in which inter-tribal marriage is a common occurrence.

Self-identification as we are seeing over the last few decades is problematic. In many cases mixed persons sometimes have to choose their tribal affiliation or enrollment, usually because governmental policy only allows that they be a member of only one tribe. As we can see as well in some cases two linguistically distinct groups can form a tribe as in the case of the Seminole Tribe of Florida, which has both Muskogee as well as Mikasuki speakers as members. Often missed by the same governmental policies broached above is that some tribal groups can be heterogeneous because of various factors besides those mentioned so far, not only because of cultural changes which have occurred as the these communities have come into contact with the mainstream social milieu. An examination of history shows many tribes which formed from previously unorganized and disparate groups which responded to the external pressure of the changing social landscape, i.e., colonization by others or the expansion of modern nations into their lands. Again the Seminole are a good example of such reorganizational responses. Because of such issues as these associated with the idea of "tribe", the majority of anthropological geneticists don't use the term as often as in the past.

The difficulty in nailing down the essence of identity in many of its even commonest manifestations is no easy task. Making this even more challenging when attempting to measure the changes to the idea and practice of identity is that so many people today view culture and ethnic identity as fluid and malleable. Thomas Eriksen is an instrumental theorist, and he is one who sees identity in these hard to accurately define terms, yet who has attempted to despite the challenge. According to Eriksen's assertion in the instrumental theoretical framework, ethnicity and identity can be explained in this direct quote from his work.

"Although ethnicity is widely believed to express cultural differences, there is variable and complex relationship between ethnicity and culture; and there is certainly no one-to-one relationship between ethnic differences and cultural ones."

People who have traveled in different tribal communities see this easily across the spectrum of Native American identities. Eriksen further speaks to the social distance realities that influence many communities.

"Ethnicity is a property of a relationship between two or several groups, not a property of a group; it exists between and not within groups."

"Ethnicity is the enduring and systematic communication of cultural differences between groups considering themselves to be distinct. It

Genetic Genealogy: A Powerful Synthesis

appears whenever cultural differences are made relevant in social interaction, and it should thus be studied at level of social life, not at the level of symbolic culture."

As witnesses to the communication between groups that today is more accessible than ever, the increased ability to perceive what differences do exist may in fact diminish some of them. Eriksen shows that ethnicity is relational and situational. As he puts it, the ethnic character of a social encounter is contingent on the situation. The nature of the encounter is not inherent. The same perspectives could well be applicable to racial identity. If we consider the word 'ethnicity' as 'identity' and 'culture' in terms of 'gene' to characterize the relational interactions between someone's identity and the genetic variation present, we gain some insights.

As we have forwarded earlier, there is quite a lot of variation and a relationship of great complexity between human genetic variation and their identity. A professor once told me to beware of simplistic explanations for complex phenomenon, and genetic variation in relation to identity is such a case, as there is no one-to-one relationship between gene and identity.

While it is well documented that 'identity' is transmitted through the systematic communication of genetic and phenotypic differences between groups that consider themselves as being distinct from others. Beside such obvious genetic variants for disease causing genes, genetic differences are made important in social interactions; the relationship between our genetic variation and our conceptions of 'race' should be studied at the level of human social life (Eriksen, 2001). This human level is our most genuine of identities.

A Nation in Transition: The 'Browning' of America

A Nation in Transition: The 'Browning' of America

The manner in which race is quantified will as it always has continue to evolve even as the American society does. The browning of America as it has been branded is a real and present reality in many segments of society. It is the future writ large for those closely observing the demographic shifts today. The Brookings Institution demographer William Frey has described the demographic changes happening as "the browning of America." Tellingly of things to come, the title of his new study on ethnicity and population change is Diversity Explosion. This is an occurrence that our generation is front row witnesses too when we think of the massive social, technological, and other changes which have happened since our grandparents childhood in the early years of the twentieth century and that of our own grandchildren in the twenty-first.

As presented in this work, the steady decline in both population size and overall vigor of America's predominant European-descended population, and its unfolding replacement by more recently arriving non-white populations from across the planet, is already underway and will not be slowing. In the present decade the white population has begun to decline across the country as a whole. His work is informative of current trends; it reveals that more than half (actually about 53%) of the United States 3,100 counties showed declining white populations by the first decade of the century presages the future.

New York and Los Angeles both are in transition to the new realities of American identity and have each lost a million whites during the last quarter century. To truly presage what is to come; statistics show that fewer than half the babies born in 2011 were enumerated in the federal Census category of "non-Hispanic whites." Most youths fewer than 18 years old will be "minorities" of one kind or another within three years. The growth of the African American population is playing a role as well, since as the census data reveals that forty years ago there were only two cities with more than a million black residents, those being New York and Chicago. Today there are seven such metropolitan areas. That Los Angeles County and adjoining Riverside County alone have more than 6.1 million Hispanic residents is just the tip of the iceberg of the emerging identities that will in a short time be the majority.

All is not new though, as the American story is based on new people, in new places, trying new things for the most part. The attitude of the author of the report that provided the above numbers has hope that this tried and true story will continue to be a resource for America, his attitude toward the contemporary social changes is much the same as the Presidents. From a demographic perspective, America is bound for greater days than ever. Frey shares his view.

A Nation in Transition: The 'Browning' of America

"Rather than being feared, America's new diversity—poised to reinvigorate the country at a time when other developed nations are facing advanced aging and population loss—can be celebrated."

Frey says that any "resistance" to the growing American diversity can be explained by Americans' trepidations.

"(Americans) fear of change, fear of losing privileged status, or fear of unwanted groups in their communities."

Then impact of the diversity of persons arriving and finding a new home is not easy to track. Defining their impact is almost as difficult as defining the arrivals identity. Since the word "Hispanic," as defined by the Census Bureau, is not a race, it begs to be defined consistently.

As asserted publicly in different contexts, though not a 'race', it is rather a designation of immigrant provenance, one that has been applied to certain individuals and groups in stranger ways as the years have passed. This label as used by the census bureau classifies people by national language, not the language of the immigrant. This is so bizarre that it is difficult to illustrate its true nature without an example. The way it is used would mean that an immigrant from the Dominican Republic is classified together with an American Indian from the Peruvian highlands, even if that Indian does not speak Spanish as many do not, and not with a Haitian who grew up ten miles away (even if that Haitian does speak Spanish). Indeed, the classifications as used are truly without practical uniformity.

To give another example of the truly strange manifestations of identity, I give the example of two friends who I worked with at a hospital in Oklahoma. One was Guillermo, called Willy by all and who had lived in the U.S. since a baby. Both his parents were Indians from a small village in Guatemala and who had immigrated to this country. Both spoke a Guatemalan Indian dialect as their first language, had later learned some Spanish, and even later learned English upon immigrating. Willy himself spoke only English, and said that he was always identified as Hispanic and himself put Hispanic as his race on forms, despite having no known Spanish ancestry.

At the same job worked my friend John, who had become an enrolled member of the Osage Nation as an adult and who said his blood quanta was "in the hundredths", sported blond hair and blue eyes, was fair complexioned and would be identifiably described as northern European in appearance. He said himself he had never engaged in any Native American cultural activities unless a couple of visits to the Indian Hospital (only to be frustrated enough to vow never to go back) could be called Native American cultural activity. My point to this story is that legally John is an American Indian and Willy is a "Hispanic" White. This example is just one of countless such situations I could recount. The classification system used by the

A Nation in Transition: The 'Browning' of America

government and society at large is not keeping pace with the diversity of identity continuing to evolve, a process only increasing exponentially with the coming years.

The American public and its wrestling match with the place that the Latino holds in the racial constructs of this country is one under constant revision it seems. Its complexity is one for the record book. The ruckus raised by Jeb Bush is one that raises a lot about popular understandings of who is counted as being 'Hispanic' and who is not. Ted Cruz, another contender for the presidency was born in Canada and is married to a 'Caucasian' woman. Cruz isn't a fluent Spanish speaker but since his father came to the U.S. as an emigrant from Cuba, and since he has surname that is Spanish in origin, his Spanish-language campaign ad in some perspectives do rightly claim that he is the first Latino senator from Texas.

Conversely, Mitt Romney has a grandfather who was indeed born in Mexico, yet since the family had lived in the United States previous to living in Mexico, this point was not made much of in the race. Romney suggested to the press that he didn't feel he was allowed to claim he was 'Latino'. That Jeb Bush's spouse and their children could be designated as "Hispanic" on a voter form without comment, but Bush himself cannot illustrates that ancestry still matters too many when it comes to who counts as Latino.

The Cherokee Paradox

The wave in social change which is increasingly spreading across the country is easily discernable in the millions of Americans who were counted on the 2000 census who changed their race, or Hispanic-origin ethnicity categories, when completing their 2010 census forms. According to new research data forwarded at the annual Population Association of America meeting, Hispanics, Americans of mixed race, American Indians and Pacific Islanders were most likely to enumerate their identity in different categorical boxes from one census to the next. University and government population scientists in this research effort analyzed federal census form data for 168 million Americans. The researchers discovered that more than 10 million individuals checked different race or Hispanic-origin boxes in the most recent federal census than they had in the 2000 census.

There are many smaller size studies which elucidate that Americans sometimes change the manner in which they describe their race or Hispanic ethnic identity. Uniquely about this study is that the new data set is the first to use statistical information from the federal census, inclusive of all Americans, to ascertain in what way these selections may vary on a wide scale. "Do Americans change their race? Yes, millions do, and this varies by group." commented co-author Carolyn A. Liebler, a University of Minnesota sociologist and one of the researchers who worked with the Census Bureau on this study. In the study the researchers did not present any hard conclusions as to the reasons for this phenomenon. Some researchers think that central to the trend is most likely how the census asks separately about race and ethnicity.

While indications are that the Census Bureau is looking into revisions of its race and ethnicity questions for the upcoming census in 2020, in an effort to better gauge how Americans think about the topic. In the eyes of some there could be other reasons, too, for the changes occurring in self-identification. The evolving phenomenon of Americans self-identity or access to benefits associated with being identified with some groups is agreed on by most as at least partially influential.

The researchers generated their estimations by matching the 2000 and 2010 census form data for the same people, following the federal Census Bureau granting them restricted access to confidential information from these censuses in return with the legally binding understanding that no details of any individual responses be revealed. Analyzing data for more than half the U.S population, including most of the 281 million counted in 2000, the researchers estimate that the amount of category-changing by responders might be even higher in the total population, they said.

Though the research documents that there were respondents of every race or ethnicity group whom changed their categories on the census form, data shows that some groups had more identification turnover than others. Most people who called themselves non-Hispanic white, black or Asian in 2000 did not change their racial categorization on the 2010 census, Liebler said. Hispanics responses were the majority in the total change, she said, but there was as well major turnover found in the responses within some of the smaller race groups as well.

The data revealed that some 2.5 million Americans who said they were Hispanic and "some other race" in 2000, (The overall largest number of those who changed their race/ethnicity category), a decade later told the census they were Hispanic and white, initially analysis shows. In contrast to this, there were another 1.3 million people made a change in the other direction, a significant group of category-changers were more than a million Americans who switched from non-Hispanic white to Hispanic white, or the other way around.

Similar to the identity struggle of Hispanics, there were more than 775,000 persons who switched in one direction or the other between white and American Indian or only white, according to data gathered. More was reported on this phenomenon in a separate paper presented at the same conference. Researchers reported "remarkable turnover" in identification from 2000 to 2010 among those self-describing as American Indian. This trend is no new occurrence though as since 1960, the number of respondents on the census who were described as American Indians has risen faster than could be

A Nation in Transition: The 'Browning' of America

accounted for by births or immigration. Changes are spread across the face of this country, with only one-third of Americans who checked more than one race in 2000 kept the same categories in 2010, according to preliminary data.

Previous research on people's racial self-identification has found that they may change categories for many reasons. Some persons who changed categories were children in 2000, young people whose race was enumerated by their parents. With the advent of the next census in 2010, they were old enough to choose their categories of enumeration for themselves, a situation which may provide explanation for some of the change. Though many people have tales of grandparents or other elders in their family being at least 'part Indian', according to a recent Pew Research Center study, only half of the people surveyed who claimed they were of a 'mixed heritage' say their grandparents or parents are of non-Hispanic White and American Indian heritage.

"This is higher than what the U.S. Census data show, the difference being that the census asks people to self-identify their own race, while our survey asked people to give the race of their parents and/or grandparents."

This insight by one of the research efforts authors, D'Vera Cohn, a senior writer and editor for the Pew Research Center, reveals the growing complexity of the identity of many Americans, and the challenge of tracking the changes occurring. While 50 percent of the responders identified their parents or grandparents of being of American Indian ancestry, most didn't identify themselves as being of a "multi-racial" identity, as only a quarter of these same responders the project surveyed consider themselves multiracial according to their responses. While 50 percent of the persons surveyed identified as having mixed heritage, there was only 22 percent who stated they feel they have a lot in common with American Indian people. Tellingly, only 19 percent of the respondents say they have had a lot of contact with their relatives who are American Indian, with 82 percent reporting that their American Indian heritage has made no difference in their lives. In the Pew study, 78 percent of the respondents who claimed Native American ancestry unsurprisingly said they cannot identify with the American Indian experience[10].

Some social media and other observers called 2015 the "Year of Self-Identification", though in some ways it may be better referred to as the "Year Self-Identification Came into Question." Like many times in the past, the courts waded into the fray of identity, with one such case be exemplary of the Terry Lee Whetstone was charged (and later pleaded guilty) to claiming to be Native American and profiting from art he sold as a Native American artist. Whetstone

---

[10] Native American Self-Identification Conflicting With Census Data, by Kerrie Fivecoat-Campbell
http://diverseeducation.com/article/79507/

met with trouble when the federal government leveled allegations that Whetstone was in violation of the 1990 Indian Arts & Crafts Act. This legislation is one which prevents people who are not enrolled members in a federally recognized tribe from asserting that their art is Indian made. As explained per the Indian Arts and Crafts Board, those who falsely claim to be Native Americans to sell art do harm to legitimate Native artists.

"(They) undermine the market for authentic Indian art and craftwork and severely undercut Indian economies, self-determination, cultural heritage and the future of an original American treasure."

Whetstone was not enrolled in any one of the three federally recognized Cherokee tribes, nor any of the other 567 federally recognized Native American tribal groups found in the United States.

Dr. Joely Proudfit is director of the California Indian Culture and Sovereignty Center and department coordinator of American Indian studies at California State University, San Marcos, a university which is among the few in the United States that serve a large number of American Indian students on its campuses. She says it is a difficult and challenging issue as to whether a student enumerating the box as being of Native American ancestry will actually facilitate educational or career opportunities.

The Cherokee Paradox

"There are a lot of problems with the system because someone may be considered American Indian for health care purposes, but not education; the federal government has some challenges to identifying American Indians. Sometimes they use the benchmark of being enrolled in a federally recognized tribe, sometimes it's the degree of Indian blood and sometimes it's the recognition by the tribal community."

Native America: Identity at the Genetic Crossroads

Native America: Identity at the Genetic Crossroads

The attempts to dissolve the identity of Native Americans by the federal government has taken countless forms across the centuries; the violence and warfare of the colonial era that carried into the young America's Indian policies of Indian removal and forced land sessions; the General Allotment Act, which destroyed communal tribal relationships with the land with individual ownership; the purposeful efforts at disruptions in Native American tribal governments in order to coerce them into the corporate Tribal Council model; the Relocation Act of 1956, intended to force indigenous peoples to move to cities and off the dwindling lands yet held; In 1953, the federal government attempted to unilaterally dissolve over 100 indigenous nations in its borders through the Termination Act. All were nails in a coffin set for a funeral for the Indian people, an anticipated death that it turns out was "greatly exaggerated". The aforementioned is but a short list of dozens of legislative acts, governmental policies, and social postures that would be the bane of tribal peoples across the last few hundred years. The arrival of genetics on the scene as tool that can both help, and hurt, Native Americans is one that one would hope could play out differently than some past experiences.

Founded on Alienation

Despite these and countless other forces at work that erode tribal identities and ties to the land there are new ones appearing unknown in generations past. The identity of the Native peoples of the Americas has been one of constant negotiations with the "other" as to the accommodation and resistance necessary to survive, and increasingly to thrive. On a human level, if our identities as individuals and communities are socially constructed, then they are not neutral some would say. Our gender, race and ethnicity, sexual orientation and class can all play an important role in determining whether we have social, political and economic power, how we employ that power, and how we respond to the exercising of it. Our identity truly shapes our life experience, how we're treated, whom we meet and become friends with, what kind of education and jobs we get, where we live, what opportunities we're afforded, and what kind of inequities we may face. For Native American people that struggle for self-determination that all these factors influence is as old as the Mayflower, and as new as the current congressional session in Washington D.C.

From the beginning, identity and religion have been connected in ways fundamental to all parties involved. From the outset the spiritual connections to the land that were foundational to tribal people's identity were the very point of the spear used to attack them. In the early part of the nineteenth century the "Nations" of the southeast were removed from lands long held by them to new lands in the west. The Christian oriented Doctrine of Discovery was quietly adopted into U.S. law by the Supreme Court in 1823 and underlies much of the relationship between Indians and the American state.

In the trendsetting court case of Johnson v. McIntosh, the relationship between Indian people and the emerging American empire would become fundamentally different than ever before, and tie Native Americans governmentally to the existence of its very colonizer. In his statement on behalf of a unanimous court, Chief Justice John Marshall forwarded unequivocally that Christian European nations asserted "ultimate dominion" over the Native American occupied lands of the Americas during the Age of Discovery. This assumption stated that upon "discovery" of these lands by Europeans Native peoples had lost "their rights to complete sovereignty, as independent nations". The communities that had been living there already for countless thousands of years only retained a right of "occupancy" in their own lands. The indigenous nations that were in the way of the steamroller of history were from the view of the descendents of these same European powers, subject to the authority of the first nation of Christendom to plant a flag and assert possession of a given area of Indian lands[11].

Upon gaining its independence from the British in 1776 the U.S. became a successor nation to the right of "discovery", and as such acquired the power of "dominion" according to Marshall, and he goes on to say (Johnson: 587-9) "discovery gave title to the government, by whose subject, or by whose authority, the discovery was made, against all other European governments." Justice Marshall cited the British charter that had been issued to the European explorer John Cabot, in his efforts to document England's "complete recognition" in his words, of the Doctrine of Discovery when he discussed the legal precedent utilized to support the Supreme Court's findings in the case.

Marshall related that John Cabot was authorized to take possession of lands, "notwithstanding the occupancy of the natives, who were heathens, and, at the same time, admitting the prior title of any Christian people who may have made a previous discovery", basing the assertions ultimately on the religious standing of them as Christians and the Natives as Pagans. With this decision by the Supreme Court, the American law that would shape the future of Native Americans would be founded on a fundamental rule of the "Law of Nations", and enshrine that to ignore the most basic rights

---

[11] Johnson and Graham's Lessee V McIntosh 21 U.S. (8 Wheat.) 543, 5 L.Ed. 681(1823).

of "heathens," and to claim that the "unoccupied lands" of Native Americans was acceptable. It gave force of law to the notions that these lands which had been home to Indian people for countless generations rightfully belonged to the "discovering" Christian European nations.

It is indeed ironic that in the same year that the Johnson v. McIntosh decision was rendered, James Madison, one of the founding fathers of the United States put pen to paper to clarify a perspective which is still at the center of American political discourse.

"Religion is not in the purview of human government. Religion is essentially distinct from civil government, and exempt from its cognizance; a connection between them is injurious to both."

Tribal people across the continent face some tough ethical questions in this age of genetic innovation and exploration. The quandary confronting tribes are as vexing as any that an individual faces. Concerning such important issues as medicine, death, and ancestry, what can individuals or tribal bodies do to maintain traditional attitudes and customary approaches even as they utilize scientific innovations to benefit themselves? These questions are now front and center for many. What happens to someone's physical remains after death and what are they giving in exchange for the data they provide that could facilitate a cure?

The Cherokee Paradox

How will the usage of genetic information affect the understanding of the identity of ancestors, as well as one's self? These are questions people across the world are asking themselves, and they are even more pressing in Indian communities, population's long suspicious of the motives of outsiders who arrive with reassurances. After five centuries of dealing with outsiders, many tribes are somewhat jaded in their response to these promises by others of benefits to come.

Everyone has an interest to one degree or another as to their origins. Figuring out where your ancestors came from is a common past time for many today. This search can become complicated and even painful when it reveals a legacy of exclusion or displacement of ancestors. Tribal communities have important cultural histories which are often times central to that community's identity. These cultural histories include their origin stories which place the people into a context on the universal level, and which are of great import in the lives of the members. Many of the tribal histories transmit a sacred connection between the people and their environment; often they relate that the tribe came from the land itself.

The more recent histories tribes hold in the internal dialogue include intruders, often Europeans and the descendants of them challenging the tribe's right to live where they did. The relationship between Natives and anthropologist is one full of contention and this has only become more pronounced in the last several years. In light of the centrality of tribal tradition in providing narratives of their roots, the perspective of many Native Americans on having a social scientist from a far off university or governmental bureau telling them where they as a people are "really" from is not appealing in the least.

*"We know who we are as a people, as an indigenous people, why would we be so interested in where (*non-native*) scientists think our genetic ancestors came from?"*

Kim Tallbear, the author of 'Native American DNA: Tribal Belonging and the False Promise of Genetic Science', and an enrolled member of the Sisseton-Wahpeton tribe and a researcher at the University of Texas at Austin asks questions relevant to the genetic sciences impacts on Native Americans. Her view of academic researchers offering to tell tribal peoples "where they are from" markedly resembles the actions of missionaries of years past, often Christian zealots unleashed into reservation tribal communities by governmental bureaucrats bent on assimilation, outsiders who came to impose on them their idea of what their religion should be. Not all tribes are against genetic testing, though, and some tribal bodies as well as countless individuals are taking part in an increasing data base of North American ancestral genetic information. Native Americans are by no means monolithic and tribes have different opinions as to the implications of genetic data to their self-perception communally.

The Cherokee Paradox

Each individual can make their own decisions as anyone can but the wrestling match which some Native Americans have professed in integrating the meaning of information as related vis modern science versus tribal traditions is for a few at least intense. A long established relationship between Native communities and those who are engaged in research, of any kind, relating to it is a good start for increasing the beneficial effect that such endeavor can have for each. Tallbear puts it best.

"I think people who want to do genetic research on Native American topics really shouldn't be doing it unless they've got a really considerable history of contact with native communities."

She goes on to put in context the reasons for the trepidation many Indians feel towards being the focus of academic research.

"You have to know something about the history, and about 20th century Native American policy, and how the U.S. as a colonial power dispersed native people from their historic homelands into urban areas and into reservations, how different groups have put tribes together on reservations who never lived together before. You have to know about relocation and post-World War II politics. If you don't understand that you can't begin to ask informed questions about the genetics of Native Americans."

Looming large on the scene of the relations between Indians and academics is the Native American Graves Protection and

Native America: Identity at the Genetic Crossroads

Repatriation Act. When the Native American Graves Protection and Repatriation Act (NAGPRA) were legislated, arguably to establish the guidelines for the treatment of Native American remains in 1990; it impacted many on each side of the issue deeply. It seems it satisfied neither adequately. It was an act which required archaeologists to return artifacts and remains to Indian tribes, sometimes for reburial without study was one which the scientific community swallowed deeply at accepting.

Those closest to the field work and interpretation of data gathered were in for a difficult crossroad; the field of archaeology had a fierce struggle among its practitioners to define the reaction to NAGPRA restrictions, and the new regulations would become greatly contentious. Concerns by many over whether they were irrevocably doing harm to their science, crippling their own field of research that has only recently become so popular in the American psyche abounded. One UCLA archaeologist described the decision to do so *"the equivalent of the historian burning documents after he has studied them."*

Is Elizabeth Warren a Native American?

Recently in the center of a storm of controversy was Elizabeth Warren, who while running for a Senate seat in Massachusetts, claimed Native American ancestry and ignited a dialogue amid the national media and kitchen tables across Indian Country about the age old question; what makes someone an "Indian"? The controversy which ensued and often ludicrous assertions by various commentators did not surprise many who live at the crossroads of identify where persons of mixed ancestry experience the ignorance of the mainstream daily.

Elizabeth Ann Warren is an academic and politician, long respected for her skillful political instinct. An uncommon woman, who as the senior United States Senator from Massachusetts has been active in the Democratic Party for years, was earlier in her career a Harvard Law School professor. Besides her acclaimed political rise, she is also a prominent legal scholar, one of the most cited in the field of commercial law by some accounts. Elizabeth Warren is regarded as a scholar of the fields of economics and personal finance. She has authored a number of academic and popular works.

Warren is from Oklahoma originally. The population of this state, a region that proudly describes itself as "Native America" on its automobile tag, and in which nearly 10% of the population there describe themselves as having Native American ancestry, has the second largest Native American population after California. The controversy emerged when it surfaced that apparently Harvard University claimed Professor Warren as a "minority" faculty member during its staff accounting processes.

Native America: Identity at the Genetic Crossroads

To the clamor of raised upon the revelation of this by the media, Warren stated that she *"was told through family lore that her maternal parents were from the Cherokee and Delaware tribes."* As any beginning genealogist quickly learns tales of the family lore as to its origins, it often is highly inaccurate and even completely false at times.

The place race plays in the lives of politicians and other public figures is always headline grabbing, as an article in the New York Times reported when Jeb Bush identified himself as "Hispanic" on a Florida voter registration form in 2009. Penned as Jeb Bush, Hispanic[12], the document created a closer scrutiny of the issue by the media. Bush tweeted, in response to a joke from his son, that it was a mistake, with the dialogue becoming the focus of the reporting as Bush was stepping into the fray of the presidential nomination campaign season. "My mistake! Don't think I've fooled anyone!" he responded on Twitter when the issue was raised in the press, with subsequent responses from his son saying "come on dad, think you checked the wrong box" and his subsequent title of #HonoraryLatino catching on.

That such mistakes could be made in filling out of governmental documents is entirely plausible in the world of red tape surrounding modern politics. His wife is Hispanic, and that someone on his staff

---

[12] (Miami-Dade County Elections Department via the New York Times)

when filling out their forms together might simply check the wrong box for Bush is understandable. That it garnered as much attention as it did in the national press was much more commentary on the election and fame of the family surname than any statement on race, one would think. Especially absent forwarded evidence by anyone that Jeb Bush called himself "Hispanic" as a pattern, a situation which the inquiries and many investigation of the circumstances of doesn't indicate was the case, Bush's assertion that he wasn't trying to claim Hispanic ethnicity seems to be the case.

The New York Times put forward in its coverage of the issue a comparison to Senator Elizabeth Warren who we looked at earlier and who claimed Native American heritage as a Harvard Law School professor, despite not having any documentable evidence of her claimed Native American ancestry. Though on some levels both Bush and Warren stumbled into the pitfall ridden world of identity politics, Warren's claiming of supposed Native American ancestry were being used as a defense of the Harvard's diversity. Contrasting to this, Bush's 2009 voter registration document was not forwarded in a context where his ethnicity would have mattered.

Cherokee Nation and Genetics

It seems from the narratives emerging from the majority of Caucasian Americans who suspect they have Native American ancestry and get tested that a great majority find no such Native

Native America: Identity at the Genetic Crossroads

Ancestry present. Upon reading DNA USA: A Genetic Portrait of America, I immediately recognized corroboration between the responses of the consumers of DTC tests I knew and those documented by Professor Sykes. He forwards the following perspectives in regards to the genetic results of several participants:

"Will's Navajo and "Roger's" Hopi chromosomes contrast dramatically with the final portrait in this room from my one and only Cherokee volunteer, "Lucas Jackson." I was astonished when I first saw his chromosome portrait, and so was he. "Isn't that something!" he said with quiet amazement. There is only one small segment of orange ["Asian" ancestry in 23andMe's ancestry painting] among an otherwise uniform sea of blue. I would have dismissed this as an error were it not for something Mike MacPherson said when I visited him in San Francisco [a scientist at 23andMe]. He had evidently had a similar experience with the company's Cherokee customers, and had often found very little sign of orange [ie., non-European] in their chromosome portraits. We did not discuss the "Cherokee paradox," as MacPherson called it, any more than that, but it did make me think that perhaps "Lucas Jackson's portrait was not so unusual for a Cherokee."

Many of the contemporary symbols of Native American identify taken for granted today by contemporary citizens have only become a part of the Cherokee culture in fairly recent times; powwow culture, flour fry bread, the ever present ribbon shirts all can be seen readily at the Cherokee National Holiday, an annual event held on Labor Day weekend annually in Tahlequah, Oklahoma. The event celebrates the September 6, 1839 signing of the Cherokee Nation Constitution in Oklahoma after the Trail of Tears Indian removal ended.

The entire aforementioned are introductions to the Indian community in today's Cherokee Nation that generation past may well have not recognized. Some cultural identifiers of earlier times, such as the southeastern Indian turban, frock coats, and even overalls (once described as the national uniform of the Cherokee Nation) would come as a surprise to some modern Cherokees citizens.

Tribal Identities

A statement from the American Anthropological Association describes the construct of race as follows.

"physical variations in the human species have no meaning except the social ones that humans put on them. Today scholars in many fields argue that "race" as it is understood in the United States of America was a social mechanism invented during the 18th century to refer to those populations brought together in colonial America: the English and other European settlers, the conquered Indian peoples, and those peoples of Africa brought in to provide slave labor. . . . As they were constructing U.S. society, leaders among European-Americans fabricated the cultural/behavioral characteristics

Native America: Identity at the Genetic Crossroads

associated with each "race," linking superior traits with Europeans and negative and inferior ones to blacks and Indians.... Ultimately, "race" as an ideology about human differences was subsequently spread to other areas of the world. It became a strategy for dividing, ranking, and controlling colonized people used by colonial powers everywhere.[13]"

The differences between notions of identity held by various constituencies in Indian country have been brought to the surface more than ever recently. Author Delphine Red Shirt, writing in the Hartford Courant forwarded that she was offended by Connecticut's definition of what it accepted as an "Indian". Speaking directly as to the reasons for her discomfort she clarified.

"Because I am an Indian... I grew up Indian, look Indian, and even speak Indian. So it offends me to come east and to see how "Indian" is defined in this state that I now call home. What offends me? That on the outside, Indians in Connecticut do not appear Indian. In fact, the Indians in Connecticut look more like they come from European or African stock. When I see them, whether they are Pequot, Mohegan, Paugussett, Paucatuck or Schaghticoke, I want to say, "These are not Indians." But I've kept quiet. I can't stay quiet any longer. These are not Indians..."

---

[13] American Anthropological Association Statement on "Race," May 17, 1998. http:// www.aaanet.org/stmts/racepp.htm (Accessed December 27, 2015).

The Cherokee Paradox

Recently Kevin Gover, the Pawnee Assistant Secretary for Indian Affairs when Red Shirt's assertions were recounted, responded in the pages of Indian Country Today.

"As I understand her position, Connecticut Indians are not Indians because they do not look like her, do not act like her, do not speak like her, do not—well, you get the picture. (They also do not have cool names like hers, but she forgot to mention that.) Expect to see Ms. Red Shirt trotted out every time some white people want to say something ugly about Indian people but dare not do so because they would be labeled as racists. I think we brown-skinned, black-haired Indians had better be careful about what we say about New England Indians. There are fewer and fewer full-bloods among us. If being Indian means looking a certain way, then most tribes are only two or three generations from extermination. The New England Indians did what they had to do to survive. They intermarried and accommodated the overwhelming presence of non-Indians. Yet they persevered and maintained themselves, some of them, as distinct social, political and cultural communities. Are they the same as the Indians who greeted the English and Dutch settlers in the 17th century? Of course not... But then few if any tribes closely resemble their pre-Columbian ancestors."

Gover's response was just one of many responses across many groups to the essence of Red Shirt's statements. Incensed letters to the Courant as well as an editorial denunciation by Indian Country

Native America: Identity at the Genetic Crossroads

Today were forwarded. Additionally Indian Country Today terminated her connection to this leading publication which she had as a columnist.

This incident, one of several I could use, illustrates the conflation of tribal identities with race and Native American identity with phenotype. Such assumptions have been par for the course in the world beyond tribal communities and from such incidents as this one do seem to be finding its way into even Indian people's views in some cases.

Although certain elements of our oft described multifaceted identity arise from certain biologically given assumptions, people most times will select and interpret the possibilities in a subjective way, and often one which is beneficial for them from their point of view. Many people construct personal meanings for themselves from these points of view garnered from particular sources, data sets that may or may not correspond with others. Identity appears to be neither completely constructed nor completely biological, as we see in the diversity surrounding us. Rather, it appears that an integrative synthesis, a blending and sorting between these two approaches happens to create the self we know.

Data available in this evolving new frontier of identity construction suggests that how people choose to integrate genetic information into their identities can influence decisions they make about testing, medical treatment, and disclosures of the results of such efforts to family members, social peers, and others. As new as this phenomenon is, especially in Indian Country, the implications of genetic identity, alongside long standing issues of tribal membership, blood quantum, and the complex interplay of the relationship with the community of identification have received little attention so far.

This fact needs future research to explore the areas I have mentioned so far more fully. It is not clear as yet how often individuals see themselves negatively due to having a particular genetic marker or the reactions they have to the information they may receive that doesn't correspond to their social identity. The degree to which individuals that do have difficult reactions to their genetic identity may be struggling is to some extent unknown, yet initially seems to be somewhat limited in number.

Admittedly still early days in this area, some previous theoretical work, while examining a multilayered construct of identity, has focused on identity as fixed in time to some degree. In contrast to this view, relationships between genetics and personal, racial and social identity can be very fluid; evolving over time and subject to multiple factors, this is an area which needs to be explored more in depth, especially in the context of the tribal cultural identity and Native American community membership.

Native America: Identity at the Genetic Crossroads

Some people who have learned at one particular point that they are of a pronouncedly different genetic origin than they had previously thought had their self-knowledge change, even if their "genetic identity" remained unaltered. They were genetically unchanged before and after learning of their results, but their perception of their own identity was transformed in many cases, and anecdotally often to their consternation.

Going forward research and dialogue within Native American community's internal discussion of genetic identity versus tribal identity should distinguish between perceived versus actual genetic identity; this conversation will be extremely difficult if past issues regarding such difficult subjects as blood quantum and tribal enrollment are any measure. The data that is coming to light on how the various multiple layers of a person's identity may in fact interact, synthesize, and influence each other. Not only can genetics shape personal identity, but personal identity can frame perceptions of genetic identity, as individuals choose which aspects of their genetics to include in their personal concepts of themselves, and how and to what degree. In regards to the distinctions made in the literature to date between individual versus social and tribal conceptions of self, genetic identity, scientific endeavor, the landscape is fast changing.

Indeed, one should think that in light of the controversies such as Kennewick Man, past exercises in Craniology and Phrenology, and conflicting perspectives on repatriation and the like, such episodes would have tainted the relationship between Indians and the scientific community even more. That people see genetic information which they become aware of as not wholly individualistic, but as something which will be affecting themselves, as well as impacting the familial and social contexts of their lives going forward is important and underserved in current discourse in native communities. These persons response to their results are multifaceted; the new information received from the DTC provider having potent emotional, familial, and potentially broader social implication in their personal standing in their community, so foundational in the context of tribal life, is logical.

The question of at what point an individual's identity may change, so much so that one is no longer oneself as previously conceived, is growing in import. The question of at what point one becomes a different self is pressing in especially on community members who were already on the fringe of the Native American community.

The persons who have utilized DTC testing and received results significantly different from their established view of themselves wrestle with the dilemma the results present. These circumstances are increasingly posing quandaries of when genetic information disrupts previous personal concepts of identity and the resultant response to the new data. The narratives that tribal members have of personal and social identity are being bent, melded, and in some cases I have been witness to broken, on a personal as well as group level. The anecdotal stories which are emerging from the Native American communities entrance into the arena of genetic identity suggest that the answer to these questions forged by consumers of the genetic information may depend, in part, on the integrity of previous narratives and the perceived relevance, public knowledge, and degree of difference from previously held concepts changed by the newly discovered genetic information.

To some degree, those interviewed did not want to become a self markedly different from that formerly conceived, but many revealed that some part of their identity had nevertheless been irrevocably altered. Those individuals with whom I have gathered information from concerning the impact on their identity post testing often present a desire for coherence in their personal narrative despite the multiple, and newly shifting aspects of their identity the results present.

Historic Definitions of Identity in Indian Country

Historic Definitions of Identity in Indian Country

How many ways are there to "be Indian"? The people of Indian country have long been caught between a rock and a hard place when it comes to identity. Defining accurately of just who is a Native American in the United States is at best a vexing topic on many fronts, and at worst a pervasive and crippling aspect of life in "Indian country". Accurately defining the meaning of terms is important in understanding how much more impact these terms and the ideas they represent have in the lives of Native American people than of those in the American mainstream. Any list of the ways Indian is defined would be incomplete without including the traditional views by Native communities of what being a part of them includes, blood quantum as the BIA computes Native descent, self-identification of individuals, and governmental definitions that can vary from program to program.

Roughly put, Indian country is any of the self-governing Native American communities throughout America, and includes "all land within the limits of any Indian reservation", "all dependent Indian communities within the borders of the United States", and "all Indian allotments, the Indian titles to which have not been extinguished.[14]" This legal classification defines Native American tribal and individual land holdings as part of a reservation, an allotment, or as a

---

[14] "18 U.S.C. 1151". Law.cornell.edu. Retrieved 2016-01-08.

public domain allotment. The entirety of federal trust lands held for American Indian tribes which are federally recognized is considered Indian country. Most federal, state, tribal and local governments utilize this category in their legal processes. According to the U.S. Federal Census taken in 2010, more than 78% of all Native Americans no longer live on reservations. The majority today are found in rural areas, towns and cities across the country.

The crux of the term Native American is based on the internal and external struggle to define who is a "Native American" for people who consider themselves Native American and for those who do not. There are many factors which have been used to define "Indian-ness," and importantly the origin and potential usage of the term play a role in which definition is used in various circumstances. This has changed often over time, and continues to do so. Some of the many aspects which characterize "Indian-ness" to many include culture, social contexts, genetics, law, and self-identification as such. An important question in this examination of the countless issues regarding our topic is whether it is possible to define the Native American identity in a concrete way or whether the definition should be one fluid and changeable in differing places, circumstances, and social contexts.

Who is a Native American? Definitions for such diffuse aspects of a concept in many ways deeply abstract may be rooted in how Native Americans respond to the dominant "mainstream" of society.

Historic Definitions of Identity in Indian Country

Viewed in some ways as an "oppositional process", a struggle by which the boundaries between the "others" and Native American communal identities are maintained, the ongoing negotiation of posture and position by Native American individuals and communities towards external and internal pressures is central to the essence of the question. The ongoing process of "ethnogenesis", the process by which the ethnic identity of the group is developed and renewed as social organizations and cultures evolve plays a major role in the defining of the multifaceted Native American identity.

According to the information the BIA forwards concerning defining Native American identity, there is no single federal or tribal criterion that establishes a person's identity as an Indian. That the federal government's several agencies use various criteria to determine who is an Indian eligible to participate in their programs is known to all who spent any time in Indian country. Generally speaking to be eligible for Bureau of Indian Affairs services, an Indian must (1) be a member of a Tribe recognized by the Federal Government, (2) one-half or more Indian blood of tribes indigenous to the United States (25 USC 479) ; or (3) must, for some purposes, be of one-fourth or more Indian ancestry. The Aleuts, Eskimos and Indians of Alaska are eligible for BIA services by legislative and administrative decision, as well. The majority of federal services and programs available, however, are limited to Indians living on or near Indian reservations.

The Cherokee Paradox

"There is no universally accepted definition of the term
'Indian.'...Although there is one ethnological definition of Indian,
there are many legal definitions...Many federal laws use the word
"Indian' without defining it. This allows federal agencies to decide
who is an Indian under those laws. Some agencies have been
accused of defining Indian too narrowly, thereby depriving people of
benefits that Congress intended them to receive. When Congress has
not defined the term, courts have used a two-part test to determine
who is an Indian. First, the person must have some Indian blood,
that is, some identifiable Indian ancestry. Second, the Indian
community must recognize this person as an Indian...The Census
Bureau takes a simple approach to these problems. The bureau lists
every person as an Indian who claims to be one.[15]*"*

Stephen L. Pevar posits in his "The Rights of Indians and Tribes:
The Basic American Civil Liberties Union Guide to Indian and
Tribal Rights". This is an efficient approach to a very sticky problem
that seems to grow more so with each generation; as America
diversifies so does the identity of the "First American". There are
several ways which most people use to identify "Indianness",
including that held "traditionally", using blood quantum, and as
defined by governmental relationships, not to mention the most
controversial, that of self-identification. We will look a little closer

---

[15] Stephen L. Pevar, The Rights of Indians and Tribes: The Basic American Civil
Liberties Union Guide to Indian and Tribal Rights, 1992.

Historic Definitions of Identity in Indian Country

at these to get an idea of the internal and external forces which have contributed to the emerging "Cherokee Paradox".

Traditional Perspectives on Native Identity

Traditional definitions of Native American identity are an important component in the interplay of complex influences that contribute to the totality of what it means to be an Indian in contemporary American discourse. Though in years past this view was given little recognition by outside authorities and was little known, today the understanding of being Indian as viewed internally by Indian communities, rooted in communal history, language, shared culture, and genealogical ties are finding traction as the bonds of colonization begin to be removed.

There is a sense of "peoplehood" which links Indian individuals and communities to tribal traditions, places, and a shared history as a unique people[16]. The definition of whom and what is "traditional" transcends academic inquiry and a binding legal terminology in many ways. The shared language of a tribal group is seen as an important part of their identity, and preserving Native languages, is a crucial part of the struggles by many tribal peoples to survive as a distinct community.

---

[16] Peroff, N.C. (2002) "Who is an American Indian?", Social Science Journal, Volume 39, Number 3, pages 349

N. Scott Momaday, a Pulitzer Prize-winning author of the Kiowa people gives a definition that is telling of the amorphous nature of the Native American perspective on tribal identity.

"An Indian is someone who thinks of themselves as an Indian. But that's not so easy to do and one has to earn the entitlement somehow. You have to have a certain experience of the world in order to formulate this idea. I consider myself an Indian; I've had the experience of an Indian. I know how my father saw the world, and his father before him.[17]*"*

Blood Quantum

A common source of definition for an individual's being Indian is based on the blood quantum of the individual, which is most often usually in context of a tribal community, though this is increasingly not always so. The majority of the federally recognized Indian tribes in the United States require a certain blood quantum for tribal membership.

In recent years, academic scholars, lawyers, media reports, and the wider public have focused unusual amounts of attention on the tribal membership requirements for enrollment, one of which is often blood quantum requirements. In some cases from the headlines of

---

[17] Bordewich, Fergus M. (1996) Killing the White Man's Indian: Reinventing Native Americans at the End of the Twentieth Century. First Anchor Books, ISBN 0-385-42036-6

Historic Definitions of Identity in Indian Country

late, still brewing controversies over tribal membership of the "Freedmen," or descendants of tribally held slaves, in the Cherokee Nation, Creek Nation, and Seminole Nation have in some instances produced scholarly and public discussions of what it means to be "Indian" and a member of a tribe or nation.

Recent controversies in Indian Country continue to spill over into the public forum as tribal dis-enrollment controversies among tribes in California concerned primarily with gaming revenues, as well as some recently federally acknowledged tribes in Rhode Island and Massachusetts, among others, have exposed the ugly underbelly of blood quantum, enrollment, and Indian politics. There's no dream catchers, dancing with wolves or sage smoke here; its raw and emotionally wrenching controversies at their worse as tribal constituencies attack one another in the press and sometimes physically.

The increasingly common internal disagreements within tribal communities over how to define tribal memberships, situations where tribal governments have unapologetically dis-enrolled entire extended families and whole categories of members are annually growing. Tribal councils sometimes by reviewing prior tribal enrollment records, bringing amendments to their laws to redefine membership eligibility, and other such actions, are changing the way an old institution in Indian Country is being viewed, internally and externally. National press coverage as well as scholarly reports on these increasing controversies has brought the ideas of Indian "blood quantum" and that of "tribal membership" to a wider non-Indian audience on the national, and even international level in some instances.

The resulting media coverage and oft unwanted publicity has put to the test the established power of tribes to define their membership. This has generally been in the past a power the tribes held independent of state and federal judicial and political control. As calls for outside intervention have become more common in some tribal communities so have challenging conversations of the often perceived illogical mechanisms, socially unresponsive, and arguably dysfunctional processes at work in Indian Country. These are realities Indians have lived with for generations but now that there are vast amounts of money involved the calls for change are increasing.

The role blood quantum has in Indian Country is not new though. The earliest usage of the concept of "blood" to establish genealogical identity legally occurred far back in European history, and through the American experience, its roots go deep into Anglo-Saxon tribal customs which arrived on the American shores with their descendants. By the year 1200, the term 'blood' became increasingly synonymous with lineage, descent, and ancestry in association with

Historic Definitions of Identity in Indian Country

royal claims to property and power and "presages modern conceptions of "race", according to some scholars.

It is already well established in the colonial governments of North America, and would only grow from there, finding its way across the continent with the settlers. Though I covered some of this information more extensively in 'The Indians of North Florida' in 2010, I should remind readers that Virginia forwarded in 1705 a legal definition of "mixed blood", by implementing the term "mulatto" for individuals with at least 1/8 blood African ancestry or 1/2 Indian ancestry as determined by colonial, European-American authorities. The terms "Colored" and "mulatto" were legally defined by several of the fledgling states in colonial times. Most commonly it was for the purposes of restricting and limiting civil and property rights of people whose presence in the public square was undesirable.

After the Revolutionary War, the United States was officially established in its own right; treaties became an essential component in negotiating with Indian tribes as sovereign political entities. To facilitate its aims of expansion, treaties were negotiated with the tribes, for various purposes, including groups ceding tribal land wanted by the Americans. These treaties were binding and were the foundational documents which defined the legal relationship between the American government and Indian tribes. This process of gaining land at the expense of tribal nations through treaty making would continue until the abolition of treaty-making in 1871.

Authorities utilizing the terminology of blood as implemented in state governments from colonial times would continue to be used by the American federal authorities in treaty making and the accompanying negotiations. This was most often to describe people of mixed Native American and non-Indian descent. Such perspectives can be found in one of the earliest references to treaties being made with "half-bloods," "half-breeds," or "quarter bloods". The process began in 1817 to grant various benefits, usually land and money, to mixed blood individuals connected to tribal groups, though many times these persons were on the fringe of the group and as such often times were targeted as spokesmen and representatives.

The first reported intermarriage between Cherokee people and the English colonists was in 1690, and so-called "White Cherokees" were numerous by 1810. Looming large in Cherokee Nation history was the 1/8 Cherokee great-grandson of a Scots trader, Chief John Ross, who led the Cherokee across the continent to new lands in the west after the tribe was forcibly removed from its southern home lands. Such integrity by mixed blood, indeed 'thin-blood' as some called such persons with very small amounts of Indian blood, leaders is somewhat rare. The cases of mixed blood chiefs signing treaties though they represented at best only small portions of the tribe are many. The use of blood quantum terminology outlined certain treaty rights regarding specific individuals, but the terms were not extended to general membership until later times.

The concept of race as defined by blood was well established in the minds of federal government officials when the American dream of manifest destiny began to expand westward later. With the surge of the population into the far ends of the continent from the original colonies the American civilization would repeatedly come to interact with more tribal nations, and the concepts and practices of the past would be utilized time and time again.

According to writers and researchers who keep tabs on Indian Country and its always tenuous status on the American political scene, the continued use of blood quantum as a way to determine membership in American Indian tribes is having serious consequences even as this is written, to say nothing of the future.

Could the blood-quantum policies of the U.S. be anything other than genocide, a process which will at some future point end with the utter extinction of the Native people of North America? Patricia Nelson Limerick is a researcher of note and is considered to be one of the leading historians of the American West. Putting the process into a timeframe perspective, Limerick presents the process bluntly.

"Set the blood quantum at one-quarter, hold to it as a rigid definition of Indians, let intermarriage proceed as it had for

centuries, and eventually Indians will be defined out of existence. When that happens, the federal government will be freed of its persistent "Indian problem". (Limerick, 1987)"

There is a substantial observable increase in the self-identified American Indian population starting in the 1960s that has little correlation with governmental tribal enrollment data from the more than 550 federally recognized tribes. This phenomenon indicates that some Americans with a mixed race ancestry are self-identifying with being an American Indian in much greater numbers, and from my conversations and interviews with many today who are part of this increase it is rooted in a different sense of self than that held by recent generations; it is as one researcher said more from a desire to shore up a "marginal ethnic identity."

The reasons for the rise could also be in the fact Indian people have the highest rates of out-marriage to other ethnicities than any other group, and since Modernity has increased Native American urbanization which has increased the interaction some Indians have with nontribal members, especially in areas where Indian communities are in close contact with non-Indian population centers. This lack of 'social distance' is facilitating marriage between groups.

The extinction by numbers of Native Americans is of great concern to many in Indian Country, as the headlines of the last few years have shown. Recent reports state that over 60 percent of all

Historic Definitions of Identity in Indian Country

American Indians are married to non-Indians. Such an arrangement is statistically not sustainable, and without doubt has certain implications for tribal group membership as established by blood quantum, the heritage of the community as a distinct group from the general population, and the identity of future generations. To see where this trend leads is to look into a glass darkly, as Congress has estimated that by the year 2080 no more than 8 percent of the Native American population will have one-half or more Indian "blood" (Bordewich F. M., 1996).

This phenomenon is one that has accelerated with time and it raises several interesting questions about the future of the Indian identity. One important question raised by the current statistics is just how much "racial admixture" can happen before the Native American population ceases to be identifiable as a distinct group? While tribal members who are enrolled in federally recognized tribes are bestowed a Certificate of Degree of Indian Blood (CDIB) card by the Bureau of Indian Affairs, does this in itself by default become the primary identifier of being an Indian?

The CDIB and its data specifying a certain degree of Indian blood the holder is alleged to have is in a state like Oklahoma in the possession of so many people who are already not identifiable as Indian that it is the primary legal and political defining factor, even as the culture, group participation, and language continue to be socially. Because each federally recognized tribe has its own blood quantum requirements with some, like the Cherokee Nation of Oklahoma, not having a minimum quantum, and others having a more restrictive set of requirements, in some cases requiring 1/2 or more, is the future of the Indian in America a two track road leading to very different futures? The demographics of Indian Country are complex.

For any who have contact with the Cherokee people and culture, it is quickly apparent that it is one of inclusion of the outsider into the community life. The most famous son of the Cherokee Nation Will Rogers once said "I never met a man I didn't like", and this attitude of friendliness and accommodation is as true of his tribe, the Cherokee. The idea of exclusivity is not a part of the traditional Cherokee, or for that matter Indian worldview. Such an idea is a carry-over from the racial paradigm of the colonial past. Smedley remarks how exclusivity is foundational to the ideology of race. The assertion that its essence is destructive to evolving and healthy identities is clear.

"It can only be maintained by the erection of social-cultural boundaries between populations that become broad barriers against interaction between "races" that it preclude any possibility of egalitarian relationships, and lastly does not recognize or provide for intermediate realities. Such boundaries are most effective when they can be transmuted into a biological axiom. (Smedley, 2007)"

Historic Definitions of Identity in Indian Country

The realities of the impact of social distance is easily apparent when the genetic identity of tribes which are farther from non-Indian population centers are compared with those who are not. Thornton puts into perspective the impacts of exclusivity on tribal communities by observing the data of reservation-versus non-reservation-based membership criteria and degree of blood requirements which are more stringent for enrollment. The information found by his research forwards the idea that Indian tribe now located on reservations have maintained a higher blood quantum requirement; this is most likely a function of geographic isolation and the social distance it creates.

The reservations, especially those larger western ones, have in the generations since the tribes were restricted to these often marginal lands have tended to isolate the tribes of the region from non-Indians and consequently intermarriage with them. In comparison, many Eastern tribes, most often with more inclusive membership parameters have in many cases set a lower (or in the case of Cherokee Nation and many other Oklahoma tribes nonexistent) blood quantum. since their populations generally have increased interaction and intermarriage with non-Indian populations, that they would need less stringent requirements for enrollment only follows (Thornton, 1997).

The Cherokee Paradox

The final Dawes rolls of the Five Civilized Tribes contained 101,506 names, of which 26,774 were listed as 'full-bloods'. Reservation should be made of these numbers because the full-bloods numbers were overstated by the matrilineality of previous generations of Cherokee and also because some full-bloods were understated due to the governmental policy of enumerating many Indians of a mixed tribal descent as mixed blood. The Dawes final rolls also documented the presence in the Indian tribes of about 3 percent adopted whites and 23 percent African descended 'freedmen'.

The mixture of differing peoples the Dawes roll documents is significant and such admixture demonstrates the absurdity of "race" being used as a determinant of Indian identity then or today in the view of many. Subsequent events have rendered it even more untenable as any basis of "Indianness" in a relevant sense of the word. To give an example of the bizarre and convoluted nature of the subject, in "The Racial Paradox of Tribal Citizenship" by Cherokee Steve Russell states that the continued exogamy by the vast majority of Cherokee citizens leads the Cherokee Nation to claim citizens of 1/2048 blood, indeed eleven generations from a full blood Cherokee ancestor (Russell, 2006)!

As we have established, it is long been that Indian tribes define their own membership requirements. This is in some ways a double edged sword. From one perspective, tribal groups in contemporary America arguably need to manage the population increases of those counted

Historic Definitions of Identity in Indian Country

as tribal members, if only to divvy up efficiently the profits of the gaming endeavors to tribal members, as well as to facilitate the economic development in the reservation or jurisdictional community. The established blood quantum system offers a solution to defining who is on the roll and who is not. The other side of the coin is that the exponential growth in tribal gaming profits has created a somewhat exclusive and from the headlines across Indian Country increasingly narrow conception of tribal identity. Tribes trying to navigate the difficult waters of modern tribal governance face two equally difficult prospects. The first is a diminishing tribal population and/or a stricter federal court or congressional oversight of tribal laws.

Congressional scrutiny of tribal governance and accompanying identities will ultimately lead to the unavoidable result that if blood quantum requirements as currently used across Indian Country are allowed to run their course, the eventual result is termination. This is not a new term in Indian Country, as in the 1950s and 1960s some tribes were "terminated" by the federal government. These groups found that once they were engaged in the process it meant losing a federally recognized status as a tribe and subsequent benefits of that status. For all intents and purposes it ended a tribal existence.

The changes that are occurring in Indian Country since the coming of the "new buffalo" as gaming has been called by some has created opportunities on many levels, and as well serious challenges for some. The economic opportunities of tribal gaming have allowed some tribes the complex process of utilizing race-based, exclusive membership criterion for enrollment. This impactful phenomenon of gaming offers some tribes a unique chance to reject non-Indian concepts of native American tribal identity and reestablish a definition of themselves held in the past. This view is of an inclusive definition of their identity whereby the shared culture is foundational to tribal membership. The extent to which this route is taken waits to be seen though.

The challenges to identity definitions that are acceptable to the many if not all is challenging as ever. Finding what would be acceptable as a functional definition of identity, one able to reconcile cultural affiliation and self-identification, but that is mindful of exclusionary definitions based on biology would be important starting points. The exclusionary nature of such definitions is a necessary component, in order to effectively yet fairly allocates always limited federal funds and tribal resources. Any proper definition of tribal membership must undoubtedly strike a balance between inclusivity and exclusivity. The defining of a tribal identity is always in continual process that allows a changing identity not fixed in cultural constructs. It cannot be something solely inherently fixed in the human genomic story. It shouldn't be viewed as defined by blood or any other facet of biology that we as people hold, whether that is real aspects of genetics or imagined implications from the data it offers. Human identity is in so many ways abstract and not something that can be cordoned off with set and definable boundaries that never change.

Most people in the Native American community have a tale of how blood quantum has affected them when growing up, and as an adult in society its presence is one of mixed emotional. A distinguished Native American and member of the Chickasaw Nation, artist Kristen Dorsey spoke recently of struggles that like many I spoke to across Indian Country she herself has concerning blood quantum.

"As a blonde, blue-eyed enrolled Chickasaw citizen, I have never been a moment without an inner debate about my personal blood quantum fraction. These issues began early on when I was a small child who knew that she was Chickasaw but was afraid that she wouldn't be if she got a cut and bled out all of her 'Indian blood.' Yes, unfortunately for many a Native American identity gets rather complicated and confusing.[18] "

Although it seems to be contradictory in many ways, laws for equal protection permit the use of blood quantum to give preferential treatment to tribally enrolled members of Indian tribes. This was partly established as it is today as a product of the 1974 case of

---

[18] http://www.beyondbuckskin.com/2012/08/beyond-blood-questioning-quantum.html

Morton v. Mancari. In this case, the United States Supreme Court forwarded that a federal agency's hiring preferences of enrolled Native Americans who met particular blood quantum requirements was not in violation of established equal protection principles. The use of the blood quantum rule was not racially discriminatory the high court ruled. The Justices said that it served the promotion of American Indians' right of self-determination. This right of self-determination for Indian tribes should not be used to insulate a tribe or to promote racially discrimination or to deny an individual the equal protection of the law though.

Though not true for all, most tribes require Indian ancestry as a requirement for membership, though there a few which due to their unique histories as tribal groups have enrolled members who do not have Native American ancestry; one example are tribal members known as the "Freedmen". These are persons who descend from slaves held by the tribes earlier in their history and in some cases have incorporated them into the tribal body. That some people of African descent have been recognized as members of Native American nations without necessarily having any Native blood isn't surprising in view of the tribal histories involved. They are for the most part descendants of the slaves of the "Five Tribes", groups originally from the Southeast and inclusive of the Cherokee, Seminole, Creek, Choctaw and Chickasaw Nations.

Historic Definitions of Identity in Indian Country

Called "civilized" by American authorities after settling down to farm and frequent the warpath less, the more prosperous and often mixed blood members copied the Southern plantation way of life. Despite this emulation of their American neighbors, they were nonetheless removed from the South in the 1830s on the Trail of Tears. Exiled to the west, most of these tribes carried their slaves with them. Both groups suffered on the difficult and arduous journey to Indian Territory, now a part of Oklahoma. During the American Civil War, portions of these same tribes supported the Confederacy and upon the defeat of the South, were punished along with the loyal portions. Large tracts of land were seized in this punishment. The federal government then drafted treaties in 1866 which required the tribes to free their slaves and make them and their descendant's tribal members.

The Indian Reorganization Act of 1934 was important in shaping the modern organizational structures of many tribes, and this legislation set up three criteria; tribal membership, ancestral descent, and blood quantum. This legislation and its subsequent manifestations in tribal governance were very influential in the use blood quantum to restrict the definition of who was considered an Indian and eligible for tribal enrollment.

Blood quantum is often viewed negatively by many in Indian communities as an imposition of external control; as Native

Americans marry out to other ethnic and racial groups at a higher rate than any other American racial category this concern is becoming more pronounced. The phenomenon of decreasing blood quantum across Indian country is a source of great debate within and outside of Indian communities and from some perspectives could lead to the eventual dissolution and assimilation of Native Americans into the larger body of multiracial mainstream American society[19] and facilitate a loss of identity as a distinct people (Peroff, 1997).

Governmental Definitions

That there is a link between the complex social identity of Native Americans and the political status they hold as enrolled members of a tribe is clear. There are over 560 federally recognized tribal groups across the United States today and, these tribes governments are acknowledged as all possessing the right to establish their own legal requirements for membership, this right having been upheld by the American Supreme Court in a case entitled Santa Clara Pueblo v. Martinez in 1978. Most often uses of the term "Indian" contemporarily utilized relate to the "political" definition of identifying as Indian individuals who are enrolled members of federally recognized tribes. The link between the components of contemporary Native identity in a legal sense is the two-part

---

[19] Peroff (1997) p487 gives the rate of interracial marriage for Native Americans as 75%, whites as 5% and blacks as 8%

Historic Definitions of Identity in Indian Country

perspective that an "Indian" is someone who is a member of an Indian tribe and an "Indian tribe" is any tribe, band, nation, or organized Indian community recognized by the United States.

This definition is preferred by governmental agencies of the federal government as well as that of tribes because it allows the tribal authorities to establish the meaning of "Indianness" in their own membership criteria. There is some pronounced criticism of this definition due to the federal government's role regarding the U. S. government and Indian tribe's relationship. Indeed, in imposing certain federal prerequisites on the nature of tribal membership requirements tribes use, this definition does not sufficiently acknowledge federal government's influence in the process, and mitigates it as one that is accurately defining of Indian identity comprehensively. In many ways there is a spectrum of sorts in this arena, where in someone who is enrolled in a federally recognized tribe has greater claim to a Native American identity, a recognition that those who claim Native American identity yet are not enrolled simply do not have. As an anthropologist who works for the BIA Office of Federal Acknowledgement stated concerning those who seek membership, the issue is sometimes illogical.

"We check and find that they haven't a trace of Indian ancestry, yet they are still totally convinced that they are Indians. Even if you have a trace of Indian blood, why do you want to select that for your

identity, and not your Irish or Italian? It's not clear why, but at this point in time, a lot of people want to be Indian." (Bordewich, 1996)

This recent surge in Americans who "want to be Indian" is at the heart of the Cherokee Paradox. One leading example of the insertion of federal authority into the defining process of Native American identity is the Arts and Crafts Act of 1990. This legislation attempts to take into consideration the limits of some definitions used in federally recognized tribal membership. In the art world, the use of Native American tribal membership is not a simple matter, as having the status of being enrolled in a state-recognized Indian tribe, as well as some artists whom have tribal recognition as an "Indian artisan" without actually possessing tribal membership. The graded categories in some aspects allows artists who identify as Indian to label legally speaking their artwork as being "Indian made", though they are not necessarily members of a federally recognized tribe (Brownell, 2001).

"I do not question the rights of the tribes to set whatever criteria they want for enrollment eligibility; but in my view, that is the extent of their rights, to say who is an enrolled Seneca or Mohawk or Navajo or Cheyenne or any other tribe. Since there are mixed bloods with enrollment numbers and some of those with very small percentages of genetic Indian ancestry, I don't feel they have the right to say to those of us without enrollment numbers that we are not of Indian heritage, only that we are not enrolled.... To say that I

am not [Indian] and to prosecute me for telling people of my Indian heritage is to deny me some of my civil liberties...and constitutes racial discrimination"

This perspective, forwarded by one Indian artist, whose mother is not Indian but whose father is Seneca and who was raised on a Seneca reservation, is indicative of the extremely complex nature of the issues surrounding even this one small corner of identity in Indian country.

Self-Identification

Most problematic of all terms used to describe an Indian is that of self-identification. In many circumstances, a person's own opinion about their identity as a Native American is sufficient to define one as an Indian. Identification as Indian without external confirmation, as when filling out the census information form, on applications to employment or to university admittance, or in public forums, is frequently exercised by those who view themselves as native American yet may lack status as an enrolled member of a federally recognized tribe.

Generally speaking, a "self-identified Indian" is someone who may not otherwise satisfy the legal requirements defining of a Native American as used by the federal government or by a particular tribe, but who sees their own identity as that of being Native American. As anyone familiar with Native American communities knows there are now many people who do not meet tribal enrollment requirements who nonetheless identify themselves as Native American.

The federal census allows all American citizens to enumerate on the census form any ethnicity they so choose, without be required of valid their selection externally. According to the 1990 Federal Census data only about 60 percent of the more than 1.8 million Americans who identified themselves on the census as being American Indian were enrolled citizens of a federally recognized tribe. This is an eye opening number, as a little less than half of those identifying themselves as Native Americans are not members of tribe recognized as such by the federal government, historically being the arguable arbiter of Native American identity, legally speaking.

According to Dr. J. Cedric Woods, director of the Institute for New England Native American Studies at the University of Massachusetts Boston, the diversity of persons and tribes not federally acknowledged yet identifying as Native American is complex.

"Most of the tribes have some degree or another of African intermixture," says Woods, a member of the Lumbee Tribe of North Carolina. "It may be a single family line. It may be multiple lines. It may be most of the lines in the tribe. It can run the entire spectrum."

Historic Definitions of Identity in Indian Country

That tribes have various eligibility requirements, often including a required degree of Indian blood to become a citizen of the tribe is well established.

"Tribes have all kinds of ... ways to determine whether somebody meets particular criteria to be a citizen of a particular government. You have some tribes who use blood quantum. You have some tribes that are still strictly matrilineal or patrilineal. You have some tribes who accept descendancy from either line. How much of that blood quantum is required is all across the map."

The growth in Americans claiming a Native American identity yet not being a member of a federally acknowledged tribe is exponential in recent decades. These persons are now becoming a very identifiable segment of the population. There are half a million Americans who receive none of the benefits of "being Indian" though they perceive themselves as such because either they are not enrolled members of a federally recognized tribe, or are members of tribal groups which have never been recognized, or they could be members of tribes whose recognition was ended by the federal government during the infamous termination policy programs in the 1950s and 1960s (Brownell, 2001).

As Kiowa Perry Horse forwards, there are many issues and elements, including ethnic nomenclature, racial attitudes, and the legal and political status of American Indian nations and Indian people, which ultimately influence Native American identity. He states that it could be viewed that there are primarily five influences on Native American self-identity at work in the identity construct of many (Horse, 2005). These would include the extent to which one is grounded in one's Native American language and culture, one's cultural identity; the validity of one's American Indian genealogy; the extent to which one holds a traditional American Indian general philosophy or worldview, one which emphasizes balance and harmony and drawing on Indian spiritual themes; self-concept as an American Indian"; enrollment or lack thereof in a tribe.

Tracing the tripling in the number of Americans who reported Indian as their race on the U.S. Federal Census from 1960 to 1990 as due to federal Indian policy, American ethnic politics, and American Indian political activism, University of Kansas sociologist Joane Nagel relates the primary forces at work in the redefinition of the Native American identity in the latter half of the twentieth century. This number rocketed from 523,591 to 1,878,285, and was most likely due to population growth, due to "ethnic switching". This phenomenon is defined as when people who previously marked as identifying as one group, later enumerate as another. Such circumstances is likely related to our increasing stress on ethnicity and personal identity as an important social construct of contemporary American society. On the long established stage on which the drama of the saga of the Native American in Modern

Historic Definitions of Identity in Indian Country

America has played out, a new and powerful force has appeared; Genetics has impacted the accepted norms and established protocols of Native America more than anything in the last century. First let's find out some of the basics of genetics.

There 'are no reports of American Indian tribes requiring or relying on DNA testing for membership' The Center for Bioethics noted several years ago and meaning such in the context for indications of Native ancestry by DNA to qualify for enrollment. The landscape began to change as genetics became more inexpensive and available though, since in February 2000, legislation was introduced into the Vermont state legislature to use the new science in relation to Native people. This act which proposed that the Vermont State Commissioner of Health should would define and bring to bear standards and procedures for DNA-HLA testing, to establish that an individual had genetic American Indian ancestry.

Though the Vermont bill failed to become law and was not subsequently reintroduced, it was significant as the initiation of the genetic data drive to be used in Indian Country on some level. It may have been defeated due to its provocation of a substantial negative backlash against the possibility of using DNA testing to establish a person's racial or ethnic heritage, either as a governmental policy or as a matter of scientific validity[20]. The above case was just one of several that erupted a decade ago as the new possibilities of genetic testing came to Indian Country.

Across the border in Canada, there erupted a controversy over tribal membership requirements in Kahnawake. This large Mohawk community is located near Montreal and is known for its stance as a community deeply committed to its tribal identity. The communities' tribal membership rules were amended in 1981 to require applicants have 'at least 50 per cent Mohawk blood'. This development was contentious and some of the reserve's people were reportedly told they could no longer have jobs or homes on the tribes reserve lands. This was to be this case even though some of those same families had lived there for generations.

After the revelations of the proposed changes to the community's membership requirements there was considerable dissention among the people of the reserve. After many divisive meetings and even some litigation, the Kahnawake community announced in March of 2003 efforts to implement change to the tribal membership rules. The leadership sought to bring about tribal enrollment reforms with the intention that while Mohawk ancestry would remain a central factor in consideration, the tribe would have other criteria as well. These would include the tribe's reserve have residency requirements

---

[20] see N Yona, 'DNA testing in Vermont', The Abolitionist Examiner, April/May 2001

and applicants show efforts to learn the Mohawk language, among others. The '50% blood rule' requirements as utilized on many Canadian reserves had been prompted by the Canadian Indian Act, legislation which forwarded the paradigm acceptant of a bureaucracy which hands down rulings from above about who is, and who is not an Indian. Professor Taiaiake Alfred, an adviser to the band council on this issue, noted the changes to the essence of tribal identity.

The Indian Act took away the fundamental rights of native people in Canada to define who they are. There is no justification outside of colonial control to have one group of people telling another group of people who they are. The object of this [new] law is to get away from the notion of blood quantum. We moved back to the traditional conception of what it means to be a Mohawk, cultural factors and community integration, as opposed to strict genetic determination[21].

These struggles over identity that are now becoming increasingly common across many tribal communities are important as languages and cultures thousands of years old and whose survival is in many cases at stake become political footballs. The unfolding story of Native Americas struggle within itself over who is an Indian is one that may be distracting from a larger question; what does the future hold for an "Indian", a member of a federally recognized tribe, and for tribal autonomy going forward?

---

[21] Tu Thanh Ha, 'Mohawk membership no longer blood simple: Quebec reserve to change divisive rule requiring strict 50-per-cent lineage', The Globe and Mail, 5 March 2003, retrieved 2 march 2015

Countdown: Extinction by the Numbers

As controversial as the thought seems, since it is the primary vehicle of legal Native American identification, the notion that citizenship in a tribal nation that is based on enrollment according to a blood quantum, if utilized as a mechanism for membership by itself is a path to certain physical extinction of the group, is a simple computational reality. Frighteningly, If we use only simple mathematics and if we know the population of the tribe, the blood quantum requirements for enrollment that it uses, the community's birth and death rates, and its rate of exogamous marriage then the date of the extinction of this tribe is calculable, from the perspective of the measurable blood quantum, used today. Tribal leaders know this, as do officials within the governments of most nation-states. Members of the tribal groups in the eastern US, whether recognized federally, recognized by states, or lacking any such acknowledgement, have seen the reality of the slow seep that is in reality the true nature of populations. They are dynamic; they change. To be static and frozen in time is not a realistic understanding of human populations, nor the Native American experience of being residents of this continent for over 20,000 years.

It is clear that regardless of the current and emerging scientific knowledge of human population genetics, utilizing such genetic information will often have difficult and impactful repercussions in

145

many cases, as Paul Brodwin a medical anthropologist at the University of Wisconsin Milwaukee who has conducted ethnographic research in the US in the fields of community psychiatry, human population genetics, and chronic pain centers and internationally in Haiti and the French West Indies makes clear.

For example, tracing your ancestry—via a pattern of particular alleles, or mutations on the Y chromosome or in mitochondrial DNA—has become not just a laboratory technique, but a political act. Who in our society requests this sort of DNA analysis, and who provides it? Once people learn the results, who controls what those results mean? It is no longer just geneticists and population biologists, but also political activists, individuals claiming inclusion in a particular ethnic, racial, or national group, and those who must decide to accept or reject their claims.

To interpret the results of research with genetic markers means not just judging whether the laboratory used the right population-specific allele or had a large enough sample size. It also involves judging the worth of genetic knowledge against other kinds of claims to authentic identity and group membership (oral history, written documentation, cultural practices, inner convictions). What is at stake in genetically-based claims of identity or rightful belonging is not just good or bad science. What is at stake is also personal esteem and self-worth, group cohesion, access to resources, and the redressing of historical injustice[22].

---

[22] P Brodwin, Genetics, Identity, and the Anthropology of Essentialism, University of Minnesota Center for Bioethics, <www.bioethics.umn.edu/genetics_and_identity/anthro_of_essentialism.html>, retrieved 12 December 2015

Countdown: Extinction by the Numbers

Blood Quantum, Allotment, and Oklahoma

The federal Indian policy in the United States has always been one that smacked of seeking the easiest route to dispensing with the "Indian problem", from some perspectives, and there are many who see the blood quantum system as a successful route thus far. It has been littered with failed policies and is marked by struggles internally in seeking the proper route to the unspoken goal of assimilation; as Roosevelt exuberantly called the federal policy of the allotment of individual parcels of communally held tribal lands; "a mighty engine pulverizing the tribal mass."

For tribal people with ties to Oklahoma's many traditional Native communities, the reality of this "pulverizing engine" is readily visible in the patchwork of Indian lands across the state, versus the large blocks of Indian trust lands still held by larger reservated western tribes. In tandem the effects of a century ago are seen in the differences in the degree of marriage to non-tribal members that is a prevalent trend even yet among many of the tribes of the Sooner State. The Burke Act of 1906, legislation which was promised to finally put to rest the affairs of the Five Civilized Tribes, is one which many Creek and Cherokee families are in some ways still dealing with.

Congress in its wisdom restricted the ways Indians could handle their portions, the alienation of allotments by "full bloods" being restricted. The unfortunate Indians who could not escape this "full blood" classification, as some did by declaring much smaller amounts of Indian ancestry than they had, were saddled with oversight of their affairs by outsiders, often corrupt ones. The act also made references to citizenship by Indian blood or the lack there of, "inter-married whites" and "freedmen" were the terms of the day found on the rolls. The Burke Act of 1906 abrogated to some degree the General Allotment Act's protective restrictions on alienation of lands.

"the Secretary of the Interior may, in his discretion, and he is hereby authorized, whenever he shall be satisfied that any Indian allottee is competent and capable of managing his or her own affairs, at any time cause to be issued to such allottee a patent in fee simple, and thereafter all restrictions as to sale, incumbrance, or taxation of said land shall be removed ".

Between the years of 1917 and 1920, Indian blood quantum was taken by the Secretary "in his discretion" as a tool for the will of the powers that be and used to mitigate Native self-determination by questioning Indian people's competency to navigate if given a level playing field.

Dennis Zotigh, an Indian and a cultural specialist at the National Museum of the American Indian a few years ago asked a Native

Countdown: Extinction by the Numbers

Hawaiian woman how Native Hawaiians view blood quantum in their culture. Her response gives a striking perspective[23].

"To the majority of Native Hawaiians, blood quantum is not an issue. We know our family bloodlines, and they are recognized by other Native Hawaiians. This is what makes us Native Hawaiian. I think blood quantum is an issue to Native Americans because of their relationship to the United States government. Native Hawaiians are not recognized by the United States the way federally recognized tribes are. Therefore, I think it is due to the government that Native Americans have to be concerned about blood quantum."

The relationship between individuals, tribes and the blood quantum system is truly convoluted. Scott Davis is the Executive director of North Dakota Indian Affairs Commission, and the situation in his family is a good example of the impractical realities of blood quantum on the lives of todays Native American families. While Scott is 44% Lakota Sioux from the Standing Rock Tribe (which requires 25% blood quantum to enroll), his wife, Lorraine, is 36% Dakota Sioux and comes from the Sisseton-Wahpeton tribe that also requires 25% blood quantum for enrollment. With the birth of their children, their girls had 39.8% blood quantum. As Standing Rock would not recognize his wife's blood, but the Sisseton-Wahpeton

---

[23] http://blog.nmai.si.edu/main/2011/09/will-current-blood-quantum-membership-requirements-make-american-indians-extinct.html

would accept Scott's, the girls were enrolled with the Sisseton-Wahpeton tribe.

A Patchwork of Red Tape

It is informative to take a look at some of the diversity in the tribal enrollment requirements for their members. As we have said tribes themselves set the requirements for membership, a foundation of the relationship between tribes and the federal government. Here are the requirements that some tribes have.

Tribes requiring a half blood quantum include:

Kialegee Tribal Town, Miccosukee Tribe of Indians of Florida, Mississippi Band of Choctaw Indians, Mississippi, St. Croix Chippewa Indians of Wisconsin, White Mountain Apache Tribe in Arizona, Yomba Shoshone Tribe in Utah.

Tribes requiring a quarter blood quanta include:

Absentee-Shawnee Tribe of Indians , Cheyenne and Arapaho Tribes of Oklahoma, Confederated Tribes and Bands of the Yakama Nation in Washington, Oneida Tribe of Indians in Wisconsin, Kickapoo Tribe of Oklahoma, Pascua Yaqui Tribe in Arizona, Kiowa Tribe of Oklahoma, Prairie Band Potawatomi Nation in Kansas, Navajo Nation in Arizona, Utah and New Mexico, Shoshone Tribe of the Wind River Reservation in Wyoming, Fort McDowell Yavapai Nation in Arizona, Standing Rock Sioux Tribe in North and South

Countdown: Extinction by the Numbers

Dakota, Utu Utu Gwaitu Paiute Tribe of California, Havapai-Prescott Tribe in Arizona, United Keetoowah Band of Cherokee Indians in Oklahoma, and the Fort Peck Assiniboine and Sioux Tribes in Montana.

Tribes requiring one eight blood quanta include:

Apache Tribe of Oklahoma, Comanche Nation in Oklahoma, Delaware Nation in Oklahoma, Confederated Tribes of the Siletz Reservation in Oregon, Fort Sill Apache Tribe of Oklahoma, Karuk Tribe of California, Muckleshoot Indian Tribe of the Muckleshoot Reservation in Washington, Northwestern Band of Shoshoni Nation of Utah (Washakie), Otoe-Missouria Tribe of Indians in Oklahoma, Pawnee Nation of Oklahoma, Ponca Nation in Oklahoma, Sac and Fox Nation in Oklahoma, Sac & Fox Nation of Missouri, Squaxin Island Tribe of the Squaxin Island Reservation in Washington, Suquamish Indian Tribe of the Port Madison Reservation in Washington, Three Affiliated Tribes of the Fort Berthold Reservation, Upper Skagit Indian Tribe of Washington, Wichita and Affiliated Tribes (Wichita, Keechi, Waco and Tawakonie) in Oklahoma.

Tribes requiring one sixteenth quanta include:

Caddo Nation, Confederated Tribes of Siletz Indians, Confederated Tribes of the Grand Ronde Community of Oregon, Fort Sill Apache

The Cherokee Paradox

Tribe, Iowa Tribe of Oklahoma , Sac and Fox Nation in Oklahoma, Eastern Band of Cherokee Indians in North Carolina.

Tribes that use lineal descent do not have a minimum blood quantum requirement for enrollment. This does not mean people with any amount of Indian blood can enroll; applicants must be direct descendants of original enrollees. Tribes that use lineal descent include:

Alabama-Quassarte Tribal Town, Cherokee Nation in Oklahoma, Chickasaw Nation, Choctaw Nation, Citizen Potawatomi Nation, Delaware Tribe of Indians, Eastern Shawnee Tribe, Kaw Nation, Mashantucket Pequot Tribe of Connecticut, Miami Tribe of Oklahoma, Modoc Tribe, Muscogee Creek Nation, Osage Nation, Ottawa Tribe of Oklahoma, Peoria Tribe of Indians, Quapaw Tribe of Oklahoma, Sault Ste. Marie Tribe of Chippewa Indians of Michigan, Seminole Nation in Oklahoma, Seneca-Cayuga Tribe of Oklahoma, Shawnee Tribe in Oklahoma, Thlopthlocco Tribal Town, Tonkawa Tribe, and the Wyandotte Nation in Oklahoma[24].

This is but a listing of some of the variations in tribal enrollment requirements, meant to give perspective on the diverse ways tribal governments legislate to exercise their right to define tribal membership requirements. It should be remembered that many of these are very different from traditional forms of community and

---

[24] http://en.wikipedia.org/wiki/Blood_quantum_laws#Implementation

tribal identification such as matriarchal/patriarchal descent, clan affiliations, and other forms.

The Cherokee Paradox: Unexpected Identities

The tradition of many white Americans of claiming a Cherokee ancestor is one that's the subject of many jokes across Indian country, and rightly so in some respects. Today, more Americans claim ancestry from at least one Cherokee forebear than any other Native American group. Across America, millions of white people tell and retell stories of long-lost Cherokee ancestors. These stories of family genealogies become murkier with each passing generation, and contemporary Americans profess their belief despite not being able to point directly to a Cherokee, or any other Indian for that matter in their family tree. Telling demographic information from the census reveals the extent to which Americans believe they're at least part Cherokee in ancestry. In 2000, the U. S. federal census reported that 729,533 Americans were enumerated as "self-identified" Cherokee. With the next census, that of 2010, that number had increased, and reported that 819,105 Americans claimed at least one Cherokee ancestor. The information from the Federal Census also indicated that the vast majority of Americans who self-identified as Cherokee, almost 70 percent of respondents recorded did claim they are mixed-race Cherokees.

The Early Cherokee Nation

Cherokee history plays a big role in this phenomenon. As European colonialism and culture engulfed Cherokee Nation during the 17th and 18th centuries, many Cherokee began altering their social and cultural traditions, in an effort to better meet the challenges of survival in their times. One important adaption to new realities was an exponential increase in marriage to whites by Cherokee. Though it is impossible to know the exact number of Cherokee who married Europeans during this period, the evidence appears that it was substantial. Cherokees viewed intermarriage with whites as a diplomatic tool and as a way of incorporating Europeans into the reciprocity that was a part of kinship in Cherokee world view.

British traders often sought out Cherokee wives and the relationships resultant indeed opened up new markets for these men; with his Native American wife providing both companionship and social entry access by Europeans to the interior of Cherokee society commenced. For Indians, intermarriage with whites made it possible for their families to secure reliable access to European goods, such as metal and iron tools, guns, and clothing. The degree with which the British reported interracial marriages among the Cherokee people testify to the sexual autonomy and political influence that Cherokee women enjoyed, as they were from a matriarchal society very different from that of Europeans. This widespread custom of intermarriage with whites soon gave rise to a mixed-race Cherokee population that appears to have been much greater than the racially mixed tribal populations of neighboring Nations.

It is without doubt that Indian ancestry is a crucial component to the preservation of Native American identity, and it is what makes the Cherokee Nation an Indian nation. For the Cherokee, like that of many other Native American tribes, history is filled with efforts to erase Cherokee identity and destroy the traditional way of life. The time over the last two centuries that the Cherokee have been in the west have been as challenging as the difficult days before removal. In writing of the Trail of Tears and its impact on the Cherokee in his work 'Andrew Jackson and His Indian Wars', Robert V. Remini reveals the depth of struggle experienced.

In a single week some 17,000 Cherokees were rounded up and herded into what was surely a concentration camp. Many sickened and died while they awaited transport to the west. In June [1838] the first contingent of about a thousand Indians boarded a steamboat and sailed down the Tennessee River on the first lap of their westward journey. Then they were boxed like animals into railroad cars drawn by two locomotives. Again there were many deaths on account of the oppressive heat and cramped conditions in the cars. For the last leg of the journey, the Cherokees walked. Small wonder they came to call this 800-mile nightmare "the Trail of Tears." Of the approximately 18,000 Cherokees who were removed, at least 4,000 died in the stockades along the way, and some say the figure actually reached 8,000. By the middle of June 1838, the general in charge of the Georgia militia proudly reported that not a single Cherokee remained in the state except as prisoners in the stockade." (Remini, 2001)

As this narrative shows, the Cherokee faced true challenges to survival. During the end of the 1800's the fortunes of the Cherokee truly fell. During the years from 1898 to1906, and beginning with the

Curtis Act of 1898, the US federal government dismantled the former Cherokee Nation's many governmental and civic institutions, with little concern for the treaties and former agreements made with them. From 1871 to 1934, Native American tribes lost over 90 million acres to white settlers.[25] The incorporation of Indian Territory into the new state of Oklahoma was underway and the Cherokee like other tribes struggling to maintain their footing as they were being swept away by the vision of American manifest destiny that was ploughing across Indian country full steam. From 1906 to 1938, the Cherokee government was little but a name, with the structure and function of the tribal government not clearly defined.

After the federal governments dissolving of the government of the Cherokee Nation in the earliest years of the 1900s, an event soon followed by the breakup of its reservation, and distribution of its land into allotments, and the future looked dim for the tribe. The Cherokee were not without leadership though, as W. W. Keeler was appointed Chief in 1949. President Richard Nixon had adopted a self-determination policy during his tenure, and the Cherokee Nation was able to begin the process of rebuilding its government. The people of the Cherokee Nation themselves had elected W. W. Keeler as chief and he was succeeded by Ross Swimmer. Continuing on its course of recovering the strength lost with the allotment, in 1975 the Cherokee

---

[25] Source: Boundless. "The Dawes Act and Indian Land Allotment." Boundless U.S. History. Boundless, 21 Jul. 2015. Retrieved 24 Jan. 2016 from https://www.boundless.com/u-s-history/textbooks/boundless-u-s-history-textbook/the-gilded-age-1870-1900-20/conquest-in-the-west-150/the-dawes-act-and-indian-land-allotment-798-1379/

drafted a constitution, formed under the name Cherokee Nation of Oklahoma, which was ratified on June 26, 1976. In a historic election in 1985, Wilma Mankiller was elected as the first female chief of the Cherokee Nation and went on to a historic career of service to her people.

Cherokee Nation Today

Today, the Cherokee Nation, as well as several other tribes in eastern Oklahoma, is a safe haven for a unique and in some ways endangered approach to identity in Indian country. Race and blood quantum are not factors in Cherokee Nation requirements for tribal citizenship eligibility. To be an enrolled citizen, an applicant needs a direct Indian by blood ancestor listed on the Dawes Rolls. This roll is at the foundation of today's enrollment process for citizenship. The current leader of the Cherokee Nation is a good example of the complex multiracial origin of most Cherokee. Principal Chief Bill John Baker was born in Cherokee County, Cherokee Nation, Oklahoma, where his family has lived for four generations, and like many Cherokee citizens his amount of Indian ancestry is very small. According to some sources, he is 1/32 Cherokee by blood, an amount similar to other leaders of the tribe in the past[26]. When I met with Chief Baker at a Native American Student Association function he was a gregarious and friendly man. Like all Cherokee Chief Baker is enrolled through an ancestor who is on the Dawes Roll.

---

[26] How much Cherokee is he?: Editor's Note. Cherokee Phoenix". June 1, 2011. Retrieved August 1, 2015.

The Dawes Rolls, which is also known as the Final Rolls of Citizens and Freedmen of the Five Civilized Tribes, or Dawes Commission of Final Rolls, was an Indian Roll created by the United States Dawes Commission, a body authorized by U.S. Congress in 1893, and formed to negotiate with the so-called "Five Civilized Tribes", in an attempt to convince them to agree to a land allotment plan and dissolution of the reservation system. This roll was ultimately utilized by some tribes when they reorganized and in some cases reincorporated, as with the Cherokee. Although there were more than 250,000 people who applied for inclusion, the Dawes Commission ultimately enrolled just over 100,000. Federal officials closed the rolls on March 5, 1907.

Some Indians, especially parties of traditional people did not apply to be included because of their rejection of the efforts to breakup tribal lands communally held, and their rejection with the allotment process. There were some others who applied but were rejected because of the residency requirements that were imposed, since many of them lived in other states. Among those who resisted a forcible inclusion in the commissions enrollment of Indians were Creek traditional leader Chitto Harjo (aka Crazy Snake), and Cherokee leader Redbird Smith, both involved in the Four Mothers Society, an organization of traditionalists resist to allotment. Though Chitto Harjo and Redbird Smith were both eventually forced into accepting the allotment, there were others who were able to avoid inclusion, including some Cherokee full-bloods living in isolated settlements in the Cookson Hills according to local Cherokee tradition.

As unfair as some viewed the allotment and the Dawes Commissions work, it ultimately became a defining event for enrolling in Cherokee Nation in future generations. Today it is a requirement for enrolling. The Cherokee Nation of Oklahoma is the largest of the three federally recognized tribes in the United States who identify as Cherokee, which includes the Eastern Band of Cherokee in North Carolina as well as the United Keetoowah Band of Cherokee Indians in Oklahoma. The roots of the Cherokee people are ancient, but the modern manifestation of the Cherokee Nation was established in the 20th century. The modern Cherokee Nation has many constituencies and includes people who descend from members of the (old) Cherokee Nation who relocated from the South due to increasing pressures from settlers there, and who came to Indian Territory as well as Cherokee who were forced to relocate on the Trail of Tears. Other constituent peoples who are part of the modern Cherokee Nation includes descendants of Cherokee Freedmen, Delaware, Shawnee, Creek and Natchez people, among just some.

Over 300,000 people are enrolled in the Cherokee Nation, with two third of them today living within the state of Oklahoma. Like its people, the Cherokee Nation itself has had much contention regarding its "corporate" identity, and according to former Bureau of Indian Affairs (BIA) head Larry EchoHawk's statement in a recent Indian Country Today article, the Cherokee Nation is not the historical Cherokee tribe but instead a "successor in interest." The land the Cherokee Nation occupies is rolling hills and flat prairie, a diverse territory across a large area. The Cherokee Nation has a tribal jurisdictional area spanning 14 counties in the northeastern corner of Oklahoma. The counties that are included are Adair, Cherokee, Craig, Delaware, Mayes, McIntosh, Muskogee, Nowata, Ottawa, Rogers, Sequoyah, Tulsa, Wagoner, and Washington Counties.

Cherokee Nation has experienced an almost unprecedented expansion in economic growth and prosperity for its citizens in recent years, with large scale projects in several districts. The Cherokee Nation currently has significant programs to provide for the welfare and future of tribal members. It is the largest tribe in the U.S., yet for its size is one with the least amount degree of Indian blood per enrolled member. For almost every tribe in the country, modernity has meant having a by-blood requirement for citizenship, and Cherokee Nation is no different. In light of recent controversies over defining Cherokee Nation citizenship, the Cherokee tribal and U. S. federal courts have upheld its sovereign right to decide who is a citizen of the Cherokee Nation.

The Cherokee Nation Supreme Court ruled in years past that citizens of the Cherokee Nation had to have Indian blood, and that fateful decision has eliminated about 2,800 Freedman (persons unable to document by-blood ancestry) descendants from the Cherokee Nation. The courts are the authority, and they made their decision after long debate and input from many constituencies. As difficult as it may be, the people of the Cherokee Nation need to abide by what the tribal courts have ruled because the double edged sword of sovereignty cuts both ways. Though the issue is still in motion on many levels and several tribal communities continue to wrestle with the place that Freedmen have in the tribal body, the issue of identity won't be settled by this one small slice of a large pie.

Tribal peoples need to ask themselves a crucial question: Who decides who is an Indian? What role does the tribal body play? To what extent does the United States government decide? For many people on all sides the issue itself is not one of racial percentages, but of how to preserve Indian identity in its many varied forms. The Cherokee Nation, like all sovereign nations, determines its citizenship by a Constitution approved by its people through legislative means. Federal courts have never told the Cherokee Nation how to determine its citizenship, and it is a fundamental right of the tribe as a sovereign nation to self-determination

Cherokee Nation is Reflective of Modern Diversity

If you come to any average Cherokee family reunion in Oklahoma today, you will most likely see a wide mix of ethnicities, as with most tribes in Eastern Oklahoma. The members of many of these smaller tribes in the area as well as the larger ones are from tribes that even upon removal approaching 2 centuries ago for some were already assimilating to some degree the culture of their American neighbors. This history shows in the phenotypical diversity of the membership of the communities.

Today, the Cherokee Nation is a complex entity that as a tribe uses documents that establish lineal biological descendant from Indians by blood on the base roll, the aforementioned Dawes Rolls. The Dawes Rolls were a federally authorized census taken from 1898 to 1914, taken in a difficult and defining time for Cherokee citizenship, since there were many people of mixed ethnicity who themselves rejected citizenship in the Cherokee nation, since the treatment of Indians was social unfair and restrictive. There were many full bloods that had their blood quantum's listed as less than they were so as not to have the required oversight and restrictions that were imposed.

Though difficult for some today to accept, the decision by that generation forever impacted their descendants, who also lost citizenship in the Cherokee Nation with that choice in some cases. As difficult as the times in that era a century ago were, in some ways they separated those who didn't have a firm grasp on their identity as Indian people tribally connected. In the words of one council person a few years ago when I spoke with her on these issues, "my ancestors chose to remain Indian and declare their citizenship with the Cherokee Nation even when others walked away from that responsibility."

The struggles over Cherokee Nation defining its membership has been contentious in the best of times and the last decade has been one with a lot of attention to the definition of who is eligible for enrollment being splashed across headlines statewide and nationally. From March of 2006 through March of 2007, the Cherokee tribal courts opened citizenship to descendants of those listed as being non-Indians on the Dawes Rolls. This is primarily two groups which included Freedmen and inter-married whites. In March 2007, Cherokee Nation citizens passed with a large margin a constitutional amendment that explicitly you had to be Cherokee Indian by blood to be an enrolled citizen. From conversations with Cherokee people in Oklahoma communities at the time, most I spoke with thought the decisions just.

When the Cherokee Nation Supreme Court ruled later, after disputes, that decision that the 2007 Constitutional amendment was valid and binding, the 2,800 Freedmen and intermarried white descendants were removed from the Cherokee Nations of Oklahoma rolls. The complexity of the layers of identity in the Cherokee Nation, as the fact that more than 1,500 Indian-by-blood Cherokee citizens who are also are descended from non-Indian Freedmen as well continue to be enrolled members of the Cherokee Nation as they always were. The meaning of being Cherokee in the modern world is truly complex. Being Cherokee is not about what you look like by any means though, as I know one councilperson that has Moroccan Cherokee cousins, folks who hold citizenship in the Cherokee Nation, the U.S. and Morocco! This isn't really unique in today's world, though. Another former councilperson told me that there were enrolled Cherokee in Japan, Germany, Korea, Israel and a dozen other countries.

Whatever the current struggles in Oklahoma between those with African ancestry and those without it, the statement that "Real Indians were created by Real White People", by Kevin Noble Maillard, who is a law professor at Syracuse University and a member of the Seminole Nation of Oklahoma is one that strikes near to the mark. The defining of a real Indian is far from the settled argument that many hope for after this recognition bill is passed, or that change in legislation forwarded. That it was able to be made into a definable A, B, or C box!

The impetus to address the impact on the Native American community of recent developments in genetics results from my own experience and growth on this journey of discovery which many are now embarked on. When I read Bryan Sykes recent book, "DNA USA, A Genetic Portrait of America" I was struck by the parallels presented by his subjects reactions and results and the people I knew who had engaged in DTC testing. He presented in his work informative chromosomal portraits of many Americans of various "self-identified" backgrounds, from different parts of the country.

Dr. Gates himself a good example of the diversity of the average American on the genetic level was included. His results which presented as half European and half African are not uncommon, and often unexpected. From the data presented other African Americans showed at least some and often times quite a bit European admixture. The racial origins of Native American groups are even more complex data emerging from the field is showing. A sample included in Brian Sykes DNA USA book was a self-identified "Cherokee", a person who test results indicated almost entirely European ancestry. The person's reaction was even keeled and logical; "Isn't that something!" Though he was unaware of it himself previously, Mr. Sykes comments in his work on the "Cherokee paradox" that is emerging across Indian

Country as more Native Americans become consumers of the inexpensive DTC kits, whose use is now becoming common.

He reports that an executive from a leading American genetic testing company shared the phenomenon that Cherokee Nation customers "had often found very little sign of orange (indications of Asian and Native American ancestry) in their chromosome portraits". This reporting of the situation he shares on page 315 of his recent book is the tip of the iceberg in some aspects. The implications for the Cherokee Paradox among many tribes such as Cherokee Nation and other extremely mixed tribal groups is that the more a group is racially mixed but nonetheless culturally self-defined by a common tribal culture, the more they grow disconnected from the complexity of their group origin. Over time they grasp for some sort of more or less mythical origin rooted in only a small portion of their genetic ancestry.

Can Genetics Tell who is Indian, and How Much?

We have been appraising how across the United States today, there is a growing curiosity about determining ones Native American ancestry that the DTC genetic testing companies are providing an easily accessible answer too. All across society there is currently a surge in the prospects of using DNA to shine some light on family stories and the like by mainstream Americans as to whether somebody is really Native American. This interest finding out more on the background of ancestors has arisen in many different circumstances since first becoming available. These contexts for finding out more can vary; determining whether ancient remains are American Indian for purposes of repatriation to tribal groups wanting federal recognition as an Indian tribe by the American government, to everyday people who believe they might have Indian ancestry and are looking for a way to "prove" it.

The promise of the new phenomenon is balanced by serious shortcomings; there are problems with using genetics to determine Native American ancestry, and it is not used to determine tribal membership in any case. The most obvious to the possibility of using this technology is the fact that being Native American is a question of legal status, of politics and of culture, not biology, necessarily. To put it most simply, and to use the legal definition that's most commonly known and used, someone is a Native American if they are recognized by a tribe as being a tribal member, if they are an enrolled citizen; Someone is not necessarily a member of any Indian tribe simply because one has Native American ancestry, even in that tribe. The requirements for tribal membership vary greatly across Indian Country, as does whether a tribe itself is recognized as "existing" under the meaning of the word in federal law. The Euchee Tribe of Oklahoma doesn't legally exist as a federally recognized tribe despite the fact that it has hundreds of members, and its own language and unique culture and a long documented history. In all other aspects it fully exists as a distinct community.

Another big problem faced by people when contemplating using DNA to clarify issues of identity is that genetic analysis, the processes involved, and social responses to the data gained. Doubtless this can be a challenge for Native American people, in terms of internal and external cultural understandings. There are aspects involved in genetic analysis that some indigenous cultural traditions consider invasive, unnatural, and in direct violation of the principles of the tribe.

Using genetic analysis to determine whether one is Native American is a point that is important but also frequently lost in the debate is that the genetic analysis itself is not conclusive, even on solely scientific terms. That the scientific shortcomings of trying to use genetic analysis to prove native identity are several is not the only challenge though. The questions involved are not just limited to the scientific shortcomings of such analysis, but includes the real legal, political, social, and moral issues involved, shortcomings emerging as we speak in some cases as new and unexpected turns in the road appear on the horizon of applying the data gathered from DTC tests to the Native American Identity.

Native American Genetic Markers in Theory

Forwarding an explanation of the theoretical framework involved in using genetics to determine Native American identity is important, as researchers have found certain markers in human genes that they label generally as being Native American markers. This assertion is because they believe all pre-Columbian Native Americans had these same genetic traits before dilution by external populations. The working theory posits that if someone has one of these markers, certain ancestors must have been Native American.

The earlier narrative stated that the genetic markers principally analyzed are found in two locations in our genes; in their mitochondrial DNA and on the Y-chromosome. On the mitochondrial DNA, there are five haplotypes, called A, B, C, D, and X. These markers are increasingly being designated as "Native American markers," believed to be the DNA signature of the ancestors who were foundational populations of Native American population today across the New World. Concerning the Y-chromosome, there are two main lineages or haplogroups present in modern Native American groups.

These haplogroups are called M3 and M45 and researchers posit that up to 95% of all Native American Y-chromosomes originate from these two groups. Though none of these markers are exclusive to only Native American populations, and all can be found in other populations around the world, they are seen with more frequency in Native American populations. We can see that the Y-chromosome and mtDNA markers are the most utilized genetic markers for analysis of someone having Native American ancestry but many people don't have a real understanding of how the process of testing for these genes work. Let's look into this process.

Native American Marker Genes in Mitochondrial Analysis

Females and males both inherit their mitochondrial DNA (mtDNA) from their mother solely, and the line of biological inheritance involved stops with each male each generation. Using a familial example, if you think of your 4 great-grandmothers, you and all your siblings have inherited your mtDNA only from your maternal grandmother's mother. This means that the other 3 great-grandmothers and your indeed your 4 great-grandfathers have contributed none of the mtDNA you would have. Let us assume we are speaking of a female in our example of the mechanics of the process. If you are a woman, you and your sisters will transmit that same great-grandmother's mitochondrial DNA to all of your own children, but your brothers won't transmit it to their children.

The Mitochondrial DNA transmitted is exactly the same as that of your mother's mother's mother, yet it does not imply a biological line of descent from the other 7 great-grandparents she would have. To put this in context of someone attempting to genetically document ties to a Native American ancestor, then if the great-grandmother we are discussing did have the genetic variations that have been labeled as A, B, C, D, or X, then by having the same Mitochondrial DNA yourself, you inherited a Native American mtDNA marker.

The process of inheritance of haplotypes is not definitive in anyway of Native American identity by any means though, since if all your other great grandparents were Indian, yet your mother's mother's mother was European or African in origin, you wouldn't have one of the Native American Mitochondrial DNA haplotypes. If this was the case, 7 of your 8 great-grandparents may well have been Native, but you would not be identified as having a Native American haplotype from the test. This example shows how as interesting and helpful haplotype based data is; despite this it is far from defining of the overall totality of the identity of the person involved, especially genetically speaking.

Native American Markers and Y-Chromosome Analysis

The way that genetics works, men will inherit a close copy of their paternal Y-chromosome from their fathers, but women have no Y-chromosome. As we have seen earlier, a test concerning haplogroups only traces a single line of ancestry. Because of this it misses most of the ancestry a person has because the vast majority of the ancestors a person actually has are unknown to the test. Like the example from earlier, if a male had 15 Native American great-great-grandparents, but his father's father's father's father was European or African, then again that person will not appear to be Native American using the test. Looking at these examples then even if almost 94% of someone's genetic inheritance is from Native Americans, under this test he may be identified as being "non-Indian". Just like Mitochondrial DNA analysis using the maternal line, to utilize Y-chromosome analysis to determine a person's Native American ancestry ignores a greatly increasing percentage of a person's ancestry as you with the analysis get deeper into generations past.

Utilization of the mitochondrial and Y-chromosome testing methods for discerning Native ancestry has already indicated how easy it can be to get a false negative using these testing techniques to attempt to establish native American ancestry based on these tests alone. If it is used by itself, there is a very high possibility of the subject having a significant amount of the ancestry they actually possess being Native American, even as they would appear to not be Native American according to the test. The assumption that in all cases all Native Americans are mono-lithic in genetic markers is another opening for getting false negatives from these types of tests as well. False negative results could conceivably arise if some Native American people simply do not have one or more of the "Native American" markers, yet are Native.

In the field of genetics, it is still early days to some degree concerning mapping the entirety of the Native American genome, and there is still much that is not known. Because genetic researchers have not tested all native people, it's not known for sure that Native Americans only have the markers they have been identified to date. The reality is that in the real world people are not bound by the researcher's ideals of genetic purity. We stated earlier that some haplotypes ascribed to Native Americans can also be found in people from other parts of the globe. A, B, C, and D for example are found in North Asia, and X is found in the south Europe and also in Turkey. Called the "9 base pair deletion," it is the principal marker of haplotype B. This marker is found in some people from Japan and is also found in almost all of the people of Samoa.

Eastern Cherokee Genetic Controversies

In 2010, a controversy erupted among the Eastern Band of Cherokee related to an enrollment quandary, a struggle that lead to talk of implementing DNA testing as a possible answer (Morris, 2010). Unlike the Cherokee Nation in Oklahoma, the Eastern Band of Cherokee historically had a blood quantum requirement for enrollment. The headlines in the community trumpeted that the "Eastern Band of Cherokee Indians is talking about moving to DNA testing as a way of verifying the blood requirement to be enrolled as a tribal member", a situation that many hoped would not become necessary, and one which many tribes are looking into and some adopting. The Eastern Band of Cherokee struggle over the results of an enrollment audit led Principal Chief Michell Hicks and some members of the tribal council to point to DNA testing as the way forward when enrolling new members of the tribe. Michell Hicks, the Principal Chief of the Eastern band gave his perspective of the possibility.

"Going forth DNA is the only way to correct this issue. I've said this from day one," Hicks said. "Council has control over the enrollment process. The chief's office doesn't have any control here. But that's always been my recommendation. If we want to get it right, let's get it right, going forward with the DNA process."

The contention within the tribal community arose when ideas of making DNA testing mandatory for those who wanted to be included on the tribe's rolls became the focal point of discussion at an Eastern Band of Cherokee Tribal Council meeting after two enrolled members from the Snowbird community asked the tribe to stop enrolling new members, at least until the auditing process had been completed.

When the Council did receive the results of the enrollment audit, it only led to more struggle over how to define the requirements to be enrolled. Ultimately an enrollment committee worked on bringing to bear the policies and procedures that would facilitate the tribe proceeding with the disenrollment of Eastern Band of Cherokee tribal members who do not meet the enrollment requirements. The audit to some members alarm showed that at least 50 people on the Eastern Band's tribal rolls didn't meet the blood degree established to qualify for eastern Band membership in the tribe, while over 300 individuals found on the roll could not prove they had an ancestor on the Baker Roll, used for enrollment today. Even in the time when the Baker Roll was established as the base roll it is remembered as a contested issue. On adoption of it in 1924, the Eastern Band's Tribal government approved 1,924 names and challenged 1,222 names on the 3,146-person roll, a considerable amount.

The audit which led to the consideration of using DNA in the vetting process for tribal membership was itself difficult on the relationships among the tribal members and their government to some degree, with some sitting council members decided to push for the use of DNA testing in the future.

"Let's start doing DNA. We've got that technology, and we need to utilize it. Instead of putting people on that aren't supposed to be."

Snowbird Representative Diamond Brown told a local paper, giving voice to concerns held by many eastern Cherokee. New found economic success by the tribe has fueled a desire by some to tighten the standards for tribal membership, a phenomenon occurring all over the country as tribes once with little resources or members find themselves now flush with both. For the Eastern band of Cherokee, each tribal member receives two checks annually as a share of casino revenue, about $8,000 a year. A complete enrollment audit and DNA testing were the only ways to save the tribe from repeating the painstaking review process again in the future some council members felt.

"The people want the rolls to be cleaned up and unless we fix the process which we're at, 20 years from now we'll be in the same boat we are in now,"

Snowbird Representative Adam Wachacha said of the perceived need for change, a change that many hoped DNA testing could help make happen.

"Everybody's got skeletons in their closets. But if we want to clean this up, the people voted on it and that's what they want to do. Those things will have to be brought out. Those things will have to be brought out in my own family."

This view voiced by Hawk Brown, a young tribal member, revealed the fact many across Indian country are learning; DNA testing sometimes can make for painful realizations for some families as to their actual origins. The struggles in 2010 by members of the Eastern Band of Cherokee and their tribal government to clarify the identity of the tribes membership using genetics is just one such effort of many.

Conclusion

I embrace the positive impacts in these amazing DNA discoveries that are coming frequently to headlines, of medical breakthroughs, amazing insights to our origins, and personal journals of discovery. The truth about our ancestors now coming to light through the field of genetics is staggering. America is more of a melting pot than we had even assumed in the past, one that we don't know how to handle the complexity of at least initially, as Professor Jennifer Hochschild told the New York Times in story in 2012.

"This is a whole new social arena; we don't have an 'etiquette' for this. We don't have social norms."

Though at first glance some may ask how important the developments in genetics really are or question the degree of impact on the lives of people it has, recent headlines give some idea of the exponential repercussions of the field on life today in many areas.

Recently after discovering that she had a genetic mutation that put her at high risk for breast cancer Actress Angelina Jolie's decision to have a prophylactic double mastectomy has raised awareness about genetic screening in the minds of many, garnering widespread press coverage and sparking debate. The incident most certainly highlights that genetic counselors can help patients deal with the psychological impact of their screening and help them weigh their options if they do find they are at risk on receiving results.

Drawbacks of DNA Ancestry Testing

Discussed more frequently of late, the attempts of many Americans to use genetic testing to prove Native American (real or imagined) ancestry is one that involves many challenges. The fact that such information if used institutionally to define "Native American" people in social, legal, or other frameworks erodes the hard won tribal sovereignty exercised by indigenous nations is just one of several poignant concerns brought to the fore by critics. Allowing a genetic test to be an arbiter of whether someone is Native American or not is to give up tribal sovereign and tribal nation's ability to determine membership is an idea rejected on most fronts in Indian country.

Though personally interesting and scientifically providing of much data that has led to fantastic insights into the history of Native Americans on the this continent over the last 20,000 years, the use of DNA tests cannot do much too concretely identify who is and who is not Native American any more than previous methods utilized in the past. The ease and inexpensive cost of DNA testing kits now being marketed to "prove your Cherokee blood" and "facilitate enrollment" as two advertisements touted recently haven't helped the already tangled web of the identity issues in Indian country.

Even on their own scientific terms, researchers have many misgivings concerning the DTC industry and its use in the "marketplace of Identity" to help people get a better picture of their origins. In part due to many false negatives and false positives possible, situations wherein they may misidentify non-Native people as Native, and misidentify Native people as non-Native, and that the positive results they do yield at best are only probabilities, no solid stock can be put in the contemporary usage of the DTC testing as defining of identity in any truly meaningful way say critics of the young science. Viewed from another perspective, if the DTC genetic kits were medical diagnostic tests, they would never be approved or adopted as acceptable by medical providers. For those seeking to find flaws in the current situation, there is plenty to address.

The DTC DNA tests in some perspectives treat Native American biology too uniformly; the approach acts as if all Indians were essentially the same and facilitates broad generalizations that may not be in the best interests of any involved. The type of testing now being marketed as definitive is indeed far from it, and to establish tribal affiliations or other information from its results is to include just part of our tribal inheritance as communities. As Native Americans, our language, culture, traditions, and personal experiences play a major part to make us, who we are, not just our genetic inheritance. The Cherokee identity is in many ways abstract, yet in a few concrete. As one Cherokee friend said to me, how much easier it would be to quantify it and control it, legislate and mandate it, and eventually the Cherokee like so many others would be a page in a history book.

It may be that because the history of identity in Indian country is so complex, its politics so convoluted, and its essence so coveted in the American psyche that it will always be a well-used tool in the hands of those with an agenda, who would manipulate it for their own purposes, even as the very people themselves who maintain it through their daily lives laugh off the circus it becomes outside of the families and communities they love. Today instead of being history the Cherokee Nation is making history. Some say that imitation is the best form of flattery. If this is the case then the millions of Americans who, unfounded or not, feel they are Cherokee, should make the Cherokee proud of the place they hold as probably the most well known and most misunderstood Indian tribe in the world.

Positives of DNA Ancestral Testing

While DNA testing overall is a relatively new technology, the many benefits of has lately caused the use of these methods to expand exponentially in a wide variety of applications. Without doubt among the most well-known benefits of DNA testing have been seen in the arena of criminal justice, Medicine, Genealogy, and even technology. In the medical world, some of the benefits of DNA testing include screening for genetic markers of future illness like cancer, Alzheimer's, or a host of other diseases. The benefits of DNA testing have led to great innovations in quality of life improvements for countless people in many ways. One example is pet owners who have embraced DNA testing for use in health care, breeding, and identification of their animals. As we have addressed earlier its long term use to determine the paternity of a child helps authorities solve legal problems and settle disputes about paternity. A paternity test is the most definitive way of determining a child's paternity. Indeed, the question of a child's paternity has never been more important, leading to new legislation in support of the child's right to know legislation in some states. As well there is emerging a growing number of sibling and grandparent tests, which can also form part of a legal case or provide data to fill gaps in a family's history.

In the world of criminal justice as well DNA testing techniques are now frequently employed to help solve murders and other crimes. When lawbreakers leave a DNA imprint at the scene of their crime they are now more likely to be apprehended, and in this new world genetic testing helps catch them. As the headlines have announced fairly frequently over the last decade many unsolved crimes have been solved due to new ways of analysis using genetic data. DNA or genetic testing has many uses that are not initially known to the public. In archeological digs, DNA tests help record genetic codes from centuries ago. This creates a data base that can be used as a future ready reference. In the world of genealogical research, genetic testing can be used to create a family tree or to clarify relationships among ancestors from a family's research project, which many now have. Through genetic data bases a person can now locate lost relatives or find relatives descended from a common ancestor. As we learned in an earlier chapter, the Y chromosome remains unchanged for generations, so people can use DNA testing to establish ancestral lines.

In the medical field, prenatal genetic tests help medical staff to determine whether or not an unborn fetus will have certain incurable health problems. Using diagnostic testing to identify or confirm an initial diagnosis of a disease or medical condition in a person or a family is now changing lives for the better, as it sometimes gives a "yes" or "no" answer in most cases. These types of tests are helpful in determining the course of a disease and the choices of treatment available. Some examples of diagnostic testing include chromosome studies, direct DNA studies, and biochemical genetic testing, to name but a few of the many now coming online.

Medicine is another extremely important area in which genetics is a powerful tool for improvements in human quality of life. With a large part of human health having a genetic basis, the struggle against inherited diseases is finally gaining some ground. While many inherited genetic diseases are caused by abnormal forms of a single or a group of genes that are passed on from one generation to the next, the use of genetics to gain insights into their processes and causes has revolutionized research in many areas. Some single genes responsible for inherited genetic diseases, such as the ones responsible for Alzheimer's disease, familial breast cancer as well as cystic fibrosis are now being isolated and characterized at molecular level. Worldwide genetic research is transforming societies.

The moral, legal and ethical dilemmas that arise as well as benefits brought through genetic screening and the new knowledge gained from genetic research, has a varying impact in each country across the globe. All approach this new world according to its own culture, political and social organizational identities and its developmental state as a nation. The response is diverse with some countries like Japan reporting a high acceptance of genetic screening and gene therapy even as other countries such as those in the Scandinavian region have a different response in some ways. The dilemmas are real and pressing in some ways as the growth of the field and its subsequent industries often outpaces the ability to regulate it. The ethical questions which are sometimes raised are beginning to find resolution at least in part.

The International Bioethics Committee of UNESCO published a draft called "Declaration on the Human Genome and its Protection in relation to Human Dignity and Human Rights" recently in light of the surging need for leadership in the area. The declaration posited contains twenty-one articles that ensure the rights of people from the point of view of emergent genetic activities. It forwarded that our human genome is a fundamental component of the common heritage of humanity, one needing to be protected in order to safeguard the integrity of the human species, as a value in itself. The human genome contains potentialities that are expressed differently according to the environment, education, living conditions and state of health of each family and each individual. By its nature it evolves and is subject to mutations and the flow of environmental pressures.

The idea forwarded that all human beings possesses a specific genetic identity and that an individual human beings personality cannot be reduced to his or her genetic characteristics is one that is foundational to our humanity few would argue. The assertion made in the declaration that each and every person has the right to be respected regardless of their genetic characteristics is a resounding international response to a new world of potential both good and bad. The clear defining of specific rights and responsibilities for everyone who participates in genetic human research, in order to help ensure human right and freedom and to allow the ongoing genomic studies to be successful is a roadmap going forward.

Adolf Hitler has always been one of the most cited examples of the dangers of using 'race' as a basis for societal policies. The outrages of his regime are well known to most people, yet comments he made regarding race can be informative. If the old adage that imitation is the most sincere form of flattery has any merit then the United States should take a closer look at the similarities to the Nazi regime and to the American past in treatment of peoples based on perceived racial differences. Hitler was in his time admired by millions and his ideologies are according to some sources on the rise again. Before World War II, he gave voice to his express admiration for the Americans handling of race.

"There are numberless examples in history, showing with terrible clarity how each time Aryan blood has become mixed with that of inferior peoples the result has been an end to the culture-sustaining race. North America, the population of which consists for the most part of Germanic elements, which mixed very little with inferior coloured nations, displays humanity and culture very different from that of Central and South America, in which the settlers, mainly Latin in origin, mingled their blood very freely with that of the aborigines. Taking the above as an example, we clearly recognize the effects of racial intermixture. The man of Germanic race on the continent of America having kept himself pure and unmixed has risen to be its master; and he will remain master as long as he does not fall into the shame of mixing the blood."

His outdated and divisive ideas about the notion of Americans as "for the most part Germanic" heritage is now being shown to be like so many concepts from the century past, ill founded. The genetic diversity that modern science reveals as having always been our heritage is coming to be much more appreciated. The 'peoplehood' of a community like the Cherokee Nation, rather than flawed ideas of race and ethnicity, are its redeeming strength, an integrity as a people that has allowed them to weather challenges of history that wiped away many others. The inclusion of others rather than exclusion of others that is at the heart of the Cherokee Identity is foundational to its success.

"Peoplehood is a community of human beings that possesses a distinct language, a particular territory, a specific ceremonial cycle and a sacred history that essentially tells how they came into existence, how they should behave in relation to their environment, when and how they perform ceremonies, and how they are related to each other within the community…" (Tom, 2000)."

The idea of "participation and memory as the basis for a tribe" and citizenship in such communities as an acknowledgement of inescapable current social realities intimately connected to traditions that antedate the United States are now gaining tractions in many tribal governments. The Supreme Court said once when speaking of the import of religion as it related to mainstream American society, that religion like identity was integral.

". . . (It is located in) the inviolable citadel of the individual heart and mind. We have come to recognize through bitter experience that it is not within the power of government to invade that citadel. "

The identity of people as they understand it is similar to this. Human identity as expressed in the Native American cultures everywhere is located not in the individual but in the peoplehood they treasure and preserve generationally. It goes without saying that it will never be within the power of the American government to invade that citadel of identity that the Supreme Court spoke of. The challenges confronting tribal communities as blood quantum continue to drop, tribal languages disappear, and social isolation continues to decrease is how to survive, and though peoplehood and tribal identity cannot be taken from the tribes, "they can surrender it in exchange for an imagined race or an illusory nation. (Russell, 2006)".

The question is, will they? Is the steady transition annually of several tribal governments' requirements for enrollment from blood quantum requirements to ones of descendancy a sign of a deepening understanding by Indian Country of its true identity and an accommodation to more expansive definitions of each tribe's essential identity? How deep into the fabric of Indian life do the hooks of colonial definitions of race and identity go? Can Indian Country handle the implications of moving forward without these fetters? As I have said the inclusion of others rather than exclusion of outsiders that is at the heart of the Cherokee Identity is foundational to its success, a success that America would do well to emulate going forward.

The question of the impacts of genetic identity in the future is open for debate. People seeking to develop some type of identity by relying upon the discovery of specific genetic markers found in their DNA test results are not finding out their identity as much as instead buying into some of the harmful premises of the eugenics movement. The danger for some people is that rather than creating their identity, from through their own relationships, they are looking to attach themselves to a communal identity. By doing this they hope to find something they can share with others based on DNA, sadly being swept away in some cases by information about ancestors more than themselves and which is a diminishing potion of their heritage for the vast number of people, even those enrolled in federally recognized tribes.

It seems that when a person pays for DNA testing, assuming to see if they show genetic markers which would be common to Native Americans, they are in the my view asserting an identity they possess as much as rather seeking a group to identify with. This is a product of the alienation many experience in modern life. Seeking ones roots is in many ways seeking ones future, and the knowledge garnered from genetics can show us how truly interconnected all are, or can if one so chooses be used to use very small differences to create more walls, more barriers, and more problems.

Bibliography

Bordewich, F. M. (1996). *Killing the White Man's Indian: Reinventing Native Americans at the End of the Twentieth Century.* New York: First Anchor Books.

Bordewich, F. M. (1996). Revolution in Indian country. *American Heritage,* 34-36.

Brownell, M. S. (2001). Who is an Indian? Searching for an Answer to the Question at the Core of Federal Indian Law. *Michigan Journal of Law Reform,* 275-320.

Eriksen, T. (2001). Ethnic identity, national identity and intergroup conflict: The significance of personal experiences. In *Social identity, intergroup conflict, and conflict reduction* (pp. 42-70). Oxford: Oxford University Press'.

Fried, M. H. (1968). On the concepts of "tribe" and "tribal society". . In H. J., *Essays on the problem of tribe.* (pp. 3-20). Seattle: University of Washington press.

Hinds, e. a. (2005, February 18). Whole-Genome Patterns of Common DNA Variation in Three Human Populations. *Science,* pp. Vol. 307 no. 5712 pp. 1072-1079 .

Horse, P. G. (2005). Native American identity. *New Directions for Student Services,* 61-68.

Lee, H. (1988). *To Kill a Mockingbird.* New York: Grand Central Publishing.

Limerick, P. N. (1987). *The Legacy of Conquest: The Unbroken Past of the American West.* New York, NY, USA: W.W. Norton & Company.

Morris, G. (2010, May 19). Cherokee enrollment quandary leads to talk of DNA testing . *Smokey Mountain News*, p. 13:19.

Peroff, N. C. (1997, February 9). Indian Identity. *The Social Science Journal*, 485-494.

Remini, R. (2001). *Andrew Jackson & his Indian Wars.* New York: Viking.

Richards, M. (2003, 2 21). 'Beware the Gene Genies: Lavish but Questionable Promises Have Been Made to Those Who Want to Trace Their Genetic Ancestry'. *The Guardian*, p. 21.

Russell, S. (2006). The Racial Paradox of Tribal Citizenship. *Indigenous Nations Journal*, 163-185.

Serre D., P. S. (2004, september 14). Evidence for gradients of human genetic diversity within and among continents. *Genome Research*, pp. 1679-85.

Smedley, A. (2007). *Race in North America: Origin and Evolution of a Worldview.* Boulder: Westview Press.

Thornton, R. (1997). Tribal membership requirements and the demography of "old" and "new" Native Americans. *Population Research and Policy Review*, 33-42.

Tom, H. (2000, April a). Sovereignty and Peoplehood. *Red Ink*, p. 43.

CPSIA information can be obtained
at www.ICGtesting.com
Printed in the USA
LVOW08s0903090717

540729LV00002B/347/P